INCONVENIENT FACTS

proving

Global Warming is a Hoax

The Common Sense Facts for the

Basket of Deplorables

Jack Madden

Preface

For years I have listened to politicians, actors, pop stars and diplomats in the UN talk about global warming. I have heard some scary predictions about bad things that are going to happen to the planet. Over a period of time I began to wonder why do these people keep on saying all of these things about global warming, when nothing that they have predicted has ever happened. What is it that they want?

I am Pragmatic. I deal with things sensibly and realistically in a way that is based on practical, rather than theoretical considerations.

So, I decided to do some investigation of my own. I began to read and research about global warming. As I studied the subject matter it became very clear to me that this is not a scientific issue, and it is not a climate issue either. Global warming is very obviously a political issue. It is a tool with the potential of great power, influence, and most importantly money! Power and influence over me as a citizen, and the power to tax my income just for using gasoline in my car, and electricity in my home.

I found that the people who are trying to convince me that I am causing global warming simply by living my life, are saying some very stupid and outrageous things. I am not a scientist, but I can recognize stupid when I see it. I don't take advice from politicians, who in my experience are more likely to be greedy and corrupt, than to be interested in my well being.

I don't form any of my opinions based on the things that pop stars or actors say. They tend to follow the "group think" mentality of the world that they live in. I love to be entertained by their movies and their music, but when they open their mouth to express their opinions, I'm out! As I said, I can recognize stupid when I see it.

If you read this book and you don't agree with me, you are certainly entitled to your opinion, and you get to live with the outcome of your choices. My hope is that when you read this you will come to the same conclusion that I have.

Global warming is not a complicated issue. It is actually very easy to understand, when you look at it through the proper perspective. I don't suffer fools easily, and I do not intend to allow stupid or corrupt people to scam me.

Jack Madden

Dedication

I dedicate this book to the glory of the Lord God almighty, the creator and redeemer of mankind. I thank my God that I was born in the United States of America, the greatest country in the history of the world, and for the freedom and liberty provided by The Constitution, the finest document ever devised by man.

Jack Madden

~ Thoughts ~

A lie gets halfway around the world before the truth has a chance to get its pants on.

-- Winston Churchill

To paraphrase Winston Churchill, I did not take the oath I have just taken with the intention of presiding over the dissolution of the world's strongest economy.

-- Ronald Reagan

Coincidence is God's way of remaining anonymous.

-- Albert Einstein

Correlation does not establish causation. Just because two things correlate does not necessarily mean that one causes the other. Correlations between two things can be caused by a third factor that affects both of them.

-- Common Sense

~ Opinions ~

"The 'global warming scare' is being used as a political tool to increase government control over American lives, incomes and decision making. It has no place in the Society's activities. As a geologist, I love Earth observations. But it is ridiculous to tie this objective to a "consensus" that humans are causing global warming when human experience, geologic data and history, and current cooling can argue otherwise. 'Consensus,' as many have said, merely represents the absence of definitive science."

-- Jack (Harrison) Schmitt
NASA Astronaut (Apollo 17 moonlanding) and Geologist
Ph. D. Geology, Harvard University

"I think the climate has been changing for billions of years." "If it's warming now, it may cool off later. I'm not in favor of just taking short-term isolated situations and depleting our resources to keep our climate just the way it is today." "I'm not necessarily of the school that we are causing it all, I think the world is causing it."

-- Dr. Buzz Aldrin
NASA Astronaut (Apollo 11 moonlanding)
Sc.D. Astronautics, Massachusetts Institute of Technology

All rights reserved, including the right to reproduce this book or any portions thereof in any form whatsoever.

Copyright 2017 by P. J. Stevenson

First Edition August 2017

For information about author interviews or book reviews, contact: emailjackmadden@gmail.com

Manufactured in the United States of America

ISBN-13: 978-1-9739-0845-6

ISBN-10: 1-9739-0845-X

Contents

ONE
What is Global Warming?   9

TWO
What Causes Global Warming?   26

THREE
What is the Evidence?   42

FOUR
Global Warming Predictions   76

FIVE
Who is behind it and What do they Want?   114

SIX
God's Solution – Earth's HVAC System   146

SEVEN
The Hoax   183

EIGHT
Al Gore – The Snake Oil Salesman   215

NINE
The Wrap Up   256

Chapter One

What Is Global Warming?

The Earth's climate has changed many times in the history of the planet. There have been seven periods of advance and retreat of glaciers in the last 650,000 years. Ice as much as one mile thick has covered all of Canada, and parts of the United States from South Dakota across the upper Midwest through New York. Each of the seven periods of warming of the climate that caused the glaciers to retreat (melt) occurred before humans invented cars, trains, jets, power plants, air conditioners or movie theaters. The end of the most recent glacial period about 11,000 years ago was the beginning of the modern climate period, and began the development of human civilization.

Global Warming in our modern era is defined as "an increase in the global-average temperature of the earth's surface", that has been observed over approximately the last one hundred and fifty years. Many of the most vocal activists who believe that global warming is caused primarily by human activities, have begun to use the term "climate change", either interchangeably with "global warming" or in replacement of the term global warming. For this book, I am using the term global warming.

When we think of "temperature", we tend to think of the temperature where we are at that very moment. Regardless of the season, the temperature will likely be different on any given day in say, Los Angeles (CA) as compared to the temperature in Chicago (IL), Miami (FL) or New York City (NY). This is because these cities are located in very different geographic locations, different altitudes, and different latitudes, and are subject to very different weather and seasonal patterns. To go a step further, the United States will have a different average temperature as compared to Europe, Asia, Africa, South America, and Australia, not to mention Antarctica.

The "global average temperature" of the earth's surface represents an average of the surface temperatures collected from all over the globe by NASA (National Aeronautics and Space Administration), NOAA (National Oceanic and Atmospheric Administration) and the Climatic Research Unit (University of East Anglia, UK) in conjunction with the Hadley Centre (UK Met Office), from land weather stations, from buoys and ships in the oceans, and from satellites. The global "average" temperature of the whole earth's surface for the full year 2016 was 58 degrees Fahrenheit (14.5 degrees Celsius).

To give you clear perspective about the global average temperature, the local temperature where most people live will fluctuate by about 20 degrees from the morning low, to the afternoon high temperature, and the seasonal swing in local temperature can be as much as 80 degrees, from start to finish of the four seasons (winter vs summer; for the full year). By comparison, the global average surface temperature will not change by more than one or two degrees over a period of time of 100 years, because it represents a huge data set that covers the entire globe, for a full year time period.

The Science community has historical global average surface temperature data going back to 1850. That historical temperature data indicates that the earth's global average surface temperature has increased by approximately 1.5 degrees Fahrenheit (0.83 degrees Celsius) since 1850. An actual increase of just 1.5 degrees over 166 years is not even noticeable, and it is hardly a magnitude of change to be alarmed about. You probably have never even heard of this actual change in the global average surface temperature of 1.5 degrees in 166 years...*have you?*

What you have likely heard is that the earth's global temperature could rise by as much as six to nine degrees, during the 21st century, IF the global warming science climate models are accurate. If that happens we are going to cook! So, it is not the actual 1.5 degree increase in the global average temperature over the last 166 years that has caused all the global warming hysteria that you have seen and heard. The northern hemisphere was several degrees warmer than we are today for thousands of years during the "Holocene" period, about 5,000 years ago. We also know that the global climate was warmer than it is today during the "Medieval Warm Period", roughly from 800 AD to 1400 AD. Clearly that was long before we were driving our SUVs, flying on jets and air conditioning our dwellings.

The 1.5 degrees of warming of the earth's average surface temperature since 1850 has not occurred in a linear pattern. Furthermore, the warming has not occurred in a sequential or directionally consistent pattern. Allow me to explain. From 1850 to 1940 the average global surface temperature increased by +1.04 degrees Fahrenheit. Then, from 1940 to approximately 1970 the average global surface temperature actually *declined* by <0.36> degrees. From approximately 1975 to 1997 there was warming of roughly +0.72 degrees Fahrenheit. Finally, from 1997 through 2016 there has been no change in the global average surface temperature. Neither higher, or lower. This is a pattern that conflicts with the narrative of the "man-made" global warming theory.

Man-made global warming is technically known as "anthropogenic" warming. Anthropogenic is defined as:

"Caused or influenced by humans". "Anthropogenic carbon dioxide is that portion of carbon dioxide in the atmosphere that is produced directly by human activities, such as the burning of fossil fuels, rather than by natural processes such as human respiration and organic material decay". We will dig much deeper into this man-made global warming theory as we move along, so I will come back to this for you.

Unless you have been living under a rock, or stranded on a deserted island with no access to modern communications of any kind, you have likely seen and heard the claims of man-made global warming that exist in our politics, in the pop culture, in the media and in the academic world. Global warming is a subject that has been featured very dramatically in many Hollywood movie productions, such as "The Day After Tomorrow" and "The 11th Hour". It has also been promoted in many very smartly produced documentaries including "An Inconvenient Truth", "Before The Flood" and "Greedy Lying Bastards". The theory of man-made global warming is widely embraced within the academic community, and is networked and advocated in the class room as well as on the lecture circuit. The main stream media almost universally embraces the idea of man-made global warming, and stories about the alleged cause and effect can be found regularly in daily news features as well as in news media produced documentaries.

Finally, man-made global warming has been widely accepted, in theory, by many leaders in the United States government, by many foreign governments, and of course by the United Nations. There have been numerous regulatory actions enacted by federal agencies (primarily by the Environmental Protection Agency) in the interest of decreasing carbon dioxide ("CO_2") emissions. There has been a great deal of discussion and negotiation in the United Nations regarding potential international treaties, with the purpose of impacting the alleged man-made global warming.

Notwithstanding all the noise about the alleged man-made global warming, no foreign government has ever agreed to be subject to any legally binding regulations regarding the control, of the growth of, or the decrease of, CO_2 emissions. The U.S. Senate voted 95-0 in 1997 to reject an international treaty (the Kyoto Protocol) regarding CO2 emissions.

Most of the messaging about global warming, whether it be by environmental activists, celebrities, or government leaders, has featured the alleged threat of future apocalyptic weather events and environmental disasters aimed at striking fear in the general public, and to influence public opinion about future decision making. However, as time has passed, the predictions of specific environmental catastrophes and climatic cataclysms have never materialized.

Global warming is a multi-billion dollar-plus per year industry in the United States and around the globe. It is a complete waste of limited and precious resources. The United States Government has been spending over $100 million + dollars of tax payer money every year on grants, research, and tax breaks for climate focused research. In addition, the U.S. government gives an unbelievable $80 billion per year to the United Nations for global climate research and foreign aid (yes, that's "billion", with a "b"). The ultimate purpose of all this spending is to influence public opinion about the existence of an alleged man-made global warming problem, to convince the public that something drastic must be done very soon to avoid an irreversible catastrophe, and to then be able to enact legislation that will result in massive taxation and life style manipulation of American citizens.

I mentioned to you previously that the hysteria over man-made global warming is not being caused by the very minor 1.5 degrees increase in the global average temperature over the last 166 years; and it is not. I guarantee you that before you read this, 99% of you did not know that the global average surface temperature of the earth is 58 degrees, and you did not know that the change in the last 166 years was only 1.5 degrees. And now that you have heard it you likely think, "ok so what?" I still need to drive my car to work tomorrow!

What you have been told is that if we don't do something to stop alleged man-made global warming very soon, then we will pass a tipping point and when we do we are going to have more super-destructive category five hurricanes, more droughts, more floods, hotter summers, and colder winters. The polar ice cap will melt, the polar bears will be extinct, the ocean levels will rise and flood the coast lines, the glaciers will melt, and humanity will not be able to survive because we won't be able to sustain the food supply sufficient to feed the world as we know it. Oh, I forgot, more F-5 tornados in Oklahoma and Kansas too.

It is as if Dr. Venkman, Dr. Stantz, Dr. Spangler and Winston Zeddemore are giving their famous speech to the mayor......"*This city is headed for a disaster of biblical proportions! (Mayor): What do you mean, "biblical"? (Ghostbusters): What he means is Old Testament, Mr. Mayor, real wrath of God type stuff. Fire and brimstone coming down from the skies! Rivers and seas boiling! Forty years of darkness! Earthquakes, volcanoes...The dead rising from the grave! Human sacrifice, dogs and cats living together... mass hysteria!*" -- Except, in the case of global warming the numerous climate disasters that have been predicted repeatedly since 1989 have never happened. And they won't.

These calamities will not be caused by just a 1.5 degrees Fahrenheit change in the global average surface temperature over the last 166 years. The predictions of environmental catastrophe are driven by the scientific computer climate models that are used by the United Nations Intergovernmental Panel on Climate Change (UN IPCC). These climate models make an assumption that the warming of the climate is being caused largely by man-made emissions of carbon dioxide (CO_2). The climate models predict the warming of the climate by as much as nine degrees by the year 2100.

There is no actual historical data to support the extreme prediction of the UN IPCC models. The UN climate models make certain theoretical assumptions that result in a dramatic escalation of the increase in the global average surface temperature, which they extrapolate as the cause of the many environmental calamities previously mentioned. The primary theoretical assumption that these climate models use, which causes the predictions of a large increase in the global average temperature, is that all the warming is being caused by the incremental man-made CO_2 emissions. As a result, as the climate models move into the future they make assumptions that cause the "greenhouse gas effect" to be compounded. This compounding of the primary assumption for the cause of the temperature warming then falsely exaggerates the future growth of the global average surface temperature. So, you get scientific mass hysteria!

There are many natural causes for global climate change that have occurred throughout the history of the earth. "Solar variations" are changes in the amount of radiant energy emitted by the Sun. There are periodic (occurring at regular intervals) variations, and there are aperiodic variations (irregular). Solar variations can cause periods of warming, and cooling. The "El Niño-Southern Oscillation" is a shift of the ocean and atmosphere system in the tropical area of the Pacific Ocean that affects global weather. Every three to ten years, the southeast trade winds weaken, allowing the warm water to flow further eastward toward South America. An El Niño warm-water phase changes global weather patterns. Another very important natural temperature variation factor is the effect of clouds. The average net effect of all clouds is to cool the global climate. Cloud changes are the least understood component of global warming, because the formation, development, and dissipation of clouds are caused by a cycle of complex and interacting mechanisms. Most climate models assume that clouds will change in ways that will increase global warming from greenhouse gas emissions. That is a very irrational assumption. Clouds block the sun. Clouds do not amplify the sun. This is pure common sense.

An entire generation of millennials are literally and unnecessarily living in fear that the earth will be incapable of sustaining the human race through their life time. They have been brainwashed from grade school through their college education by teachers and professors who, themselves, were brainwashed before them. In order to get their attention, and gain their acceptance of the theory, global warming activists have presented scary scenarios and have made simplified, dramatic predictions, so that they can capture the public's imagination by getting loads of media coverage as a means to advance the cause.

So, here is what we have covered so far. Global warming is "an increase in the global-average temperature of the earth's surface", that has been observed over approximately the last 166 years. The global average temperature of the earth's surface for the full year 2016 was 58 degrees Fahrenheit, so it is safe to say that is roughly where we are today (2017). We know based on actual historical recorded temperatures that the earth's global average surface temperature has increased by approximately 1.5 degrees Fahrenheit since 1850. An actual increase of just 1.5 degrees in 166 years is not noticeable, and in fact it has caused no harm to the environment or the climate. It is considered to be normal climate variation based on the history of the earth.

"Global warming" became the dominant popular term to be used to describe the alleged environmental effects of human emissions of CO_2, after NASA scientist James Hansen used it in June 1988 while presenting dramatic testimony to the U.S. Congress. The mainstream media adopted the story after Mr. Hansen said that he was "*99 percent sure that a long-term, worldwide warming trend was underway, and that he suspected that the greenhouse effect was responsible*" for the warming trend. At that time, there had been a period of ten years during which the global average surface temperature was on the rise.

However, there has been no warming since 1997 (20 years) even though one-third of all human CO2 emissions since 1750, have occurred since 1997. Some political maneuvering has triggered a debate over the use of the scientific terms "global warming" vs. "climate change". The supporters of the man-made global warming theory have started to use the "climate change" reference in an attempt to minimize their loss of credibility caused by the lack of warming in the last 20 years ("The Pause"). This contradicts the global warming science climate models cited in the IPCC's various reports, because not one of them predicted any "Pause" in the warming trend.

"Global warming" is the official term for this *"Inconvenient Facts proving Global Warming is a Hoax: The Common Sense Facts for the Basket of Deplorables"*. The term "climate change" is the hypocritical term being used by the man-made global warming activists, as they try to hide from the fact that there has been NO global warming in the last 20 years.

What the term "climate change" really represents is the normal variation of the earth's climate over the full 4.5 billion year history of our planet. The climate history of the earth has seen four ice ages come and go during the last 2.5 billion years, and a fifth ice age in which we are currently living. We are in an "interglacial period" of warm global temperatures. The earth is still very much in an ice age as there are many active glaciers around the world, including the very prominent ice sheets covering Antarctica (the south pole), Greenland and the Arctic Ocean sea ice (north pole). The current ice age is called the "Quaternary", and it began about 2.5 million years ago. The interglacial period that we are currently in began about 11,000 years ago.

So, either global warming is being caused primarily by human activities, or it is a normal variation of the earth's climate that occurs with regularity. That is what we are going to discuss. Global warming is not a planetary emergency. There is no evidence of an increase in natural disasters beyond what normally occurs over the planet's recorded history. There are many natural factors that affect the climate of the planet, over which mankind has absolutely no control. As you read forward I will demonstrate for you that there is no significant correlation between the modest growth in the global average temperature since 1850, and the growth in the emissions of carbon dioxide since the beginning of the industrial revolution. We know that 75% of the temperature growth since the beginning of the industrial revolution occurred before 1940, but 75% of the human emissions of carbon dioxide have occurred after 1940.

Despite what you have been told, there is no "consensus" among the greater scientific community about global warming. In science consensus is irrelevant. What is relevant is reproducible results. The work of science has nothing to do with consensus. Consensus is the business of politics.

Chapter Two

What Causes Global Warming?

The atmosphere is a mixture of gases that surrounds the earth and protects human life, all living creatures, and the planet's environment, from the extreme conditions of outer space. The temperature in outer space near the earth's atmosphere ranges from 150 degrees Fahrenheit below zero in the shade, to more than 250 degrees in the sunlight, a deadly swing of 400 degrees. The atmosphere also holds the oxygen that humans and living creatures need to breathe, close to the earth's surface where it is needed. The atmosphere provides the framework which allows the earth's natural "greenhouse effect", and the "weather systems" to maintain a livable temperature on the surface of the earth.

There is significant disagreement in the scientific community and in the political world regarding the existence of global warming, and the cause and extent of any future alleged warming of the earth's climate. The concept of man-made global warming has been widely discussed and hyper-dramatized in our politics, in the pop culture, in the media and in the academic world. I will present the argument that is put forward by both sides of this subject, and I will also unapologetically give you my very strong opinions with a common sense perspective, and you can make your best reasoned judgment of what you believe to be true about this issue.

The man-made global warming argument

The scientists that argue that there is man-made global warming, and that the warming will be more serious in the future, state that the major cause of the alleged warming climate, is the burning of fossil fuels, which is relatively quickly causing an increase of the concentration of carbon dioxide (CO2) in the atmosphere.

The purpose of the earth's natural "greenhouse effect" is to keep enough of the heat from the sunlight inside the atmosphere to maintain a livable temperature at the earth's surface. When sunlight contacts the surface of the earth, about one-third of it is reflected back out into outer space. This reflected sunlight is called "infrared light". If all the infrared light escaped the atmosphere then the surface of the earth where we live would be too cold. The greenhouse gases hold some of the heat from the infrared light inside the atmosphere, similar to how a blanket keeps you warm when you are in a cold room. The global warming scientists believe that the growth of the carbon dioxide emissions generated by human activities is causing an increase in the blanket effect of the greenhouse gases, thereby causing an alleged warming of the earth's surface temperature.

Carbon Dioxide (CO2) is at the center of the argument by the scientists, politicians and activists who believe that human activity is the primary cause of the alleged global warming. Note that, when I say "alleged", I am referring to the fact that the actual global warming that we have seen to date is within the normal historical climate variations. The extreme global warming that the activist scientists refer to is "predicted", and exists only in their computerized climate models.

Carbon Dioxide is a colorless, odorless, nontoxic gas, and it is primarily produced by natural processes of the earth. The earth's oceans, soil, plants, animals and volcanoes are all natural sources of carbon dioxide emissions. If you have ever seen the movie "Apollo 13", you know that human beings also breath out carbon dioxide when we exhale.

Carbon Dioxide is also produced by the use of carbon based fossil fuels such as petroleum products, gasoline, coal and natural gas. Driving a car, riding a bus or a train, flying on an airplane, and using electricity are human activities that cause the emission of carbon dioxide into the earth's atmosphere.

Carbon Dioxide is not a pollutant, it is not a poison, and it won't hurt or kill you. Carbon Dioxide is actually necessary for the existence of all living beings and creatures on the planet earth. When plants perform photosynthesis (the way that a plant produces its food), the plant absorbs carbon dioxide, and then releases oxygen into the air, which humans need to breath to survive. This is not my opinion about carbon dioxide. It is scientific fact that is not in dispute. "CO2" is the molecular formula for carbon dioxide. A molecule of the compound carbon dioxide contains one atom of the element carbon, and two atoms of the element oxygen. Carbon in its pure form can be found in oil, coal, and diamonds. The human body composition contains approximately 18 percent carbon.

Carbon Dioxide is also referred to as one of the "greenhouse gases". The greenhouse gases that are in the earth's atmosphere include water vapor, methane and carbon dioxide, and there are others in very small concentrations. Water Vapor comprises about 80 percent of the mass of the greenhouse gases, but it accounts for as much as 90 percent of the earth's natural greenhouse "effect". Clouds also have a significant greenhouse effect, however clouds are not a gas. Clouds consist of tiny water droplets or ice crystals, depending on their altitude, and some other factors.

The carbon dioxide that is in the atmosphere of our earth is a very small portion of the total atmospheric greenhouse gases (only about 10%). The concentration is so small that carbon dioxide is actually referred to as one of the "trace gases". The current concentration of the carbon dioxide compared to the total greenhouse gases in the atmosphere is 400 "parts per million". This means that for every one-million (1,000,000) molecules of air in the atmosphere, there are only 400 molecules of carbon dioxide. Expressed as a percentage it would be 0.04% (that is, 4 – one hundredths of one percent). There just simply isn't very much of it. If the atmosphere was a cocktail, and the CO2 was the alcohol, you would be telling your bar tender to pour harder…much harder! For comparison, the carbon dioxide concentration in the atmosphere in the year 1800 was 280 parts per million.

It should be noted that the presence of more carbon dioxide in the atmosphere is actually a good thing. The increased CO2 concentrations boost the photosynthesis activity of plants and trees, enhances crop growth, improves water-use efficiency of all plants, and strengthens plant's resistance to natural environmental stresses. More CO2 in the atmosphere is like giving free fertilizer to the poor and undeveloped nations of the world that struggle to feed their population.

In the history of the earth there have been periods of cooling and periods of warming. This is a natural process that is a part of the earth's life cycle. The global warming "crisis" movement that is popularized by some famous people including Al Gore, Leonardo DiCaprio, and Barack Obama, theorizes that the human emissions of carbon dioxide since the beginning of the industrial revolution (which started about 1820) has caused a significant increase in carbon dioxide emissions, which is fueling a warming of the earth's temperature, and causing other alleged problems and anomalies in the climate worldwide.

The problem with that theory is that the earth's climate has not behaved in a linear pattern since 1850. Despite the fact that the level of carbon dioxide emissions has been constantly increasing during the last 166 years, due to the growth of the world's population, and the industrialization of many developing countries around the world that is driven by the advent of technology, there have been clearly documented periods of warming and cooling in recent history. For example, during the period from 1850 – 1940, the earth's average temperature warmed by about 1.04 degrees Fahrenheit. Then during the period from 1940–1970, the earth's average temperature *cooled* by about 0.36 degrees Fahrenheit. From 1975 to 1997 there was warming of approximately 0.72 degrees Fahrenheit. Since 1997, there has been no change in the earth's average surface temperature, a period of 20 years.

This recent 20-year period with no current global warming of the surface temperature is now as long as the prior period of warming, despite the fact that human activities in the world have produced even more emissions of the very carbon dioxide that is supposed to be the predominant cause of the alleged global warming.

One-third of all carbon dioxide produced in the world since the beginning of the industrial revolution has occurred since 1997. During this time there has been *no further warming.* From a perspective of common sense, it appears that there is no direct correlation between the growth in human caused carbon dioxide emissions, and the movement (up or down) of the earth's climate. Or, at the very least, any correlation that may exist is outweighed by powerful counter-acting natural processes occurring in the climate and extraordinary forces upon the planet from the solar system.

The truth is that the earth has basically been starved of carbon dioxide. We know that carbon dioxide is essential for life on earth, as it feeds plant life and fuels photosynthesis, which then provides the oxygen that humans and animals need to breath. The increase in the carbon dioxide in the atmosphere has actually increased agricultural growth and output worldwide causing a greening of the planet. This in turn has helped to feed the growing human population, particularly in some of the poorer areas of the globe.

We know that there has been some overall warming of the earth's climate, of about 1.5 degrees Fahrenheit since 1850. An increase of 1.5 degrees in a period of 166 years is well within the normal range of climate variance in the earth's history. There has not been any pattern of global disasters, threatening a planetary crisis, causing a complete or even significant melting of the Arctic Sea Ice, or causing catastrophic rising of sea levels, as have been famously predicted by Al Gore and Barack Obama repeatedly since 1995 and 2006, respectively.

What we have seen is the normal pattern of weather and climate variations, including some years of mild seasonal weather and some years of extreme weather events, on a regional and localized basis. There has been the occasional season of hurricanes of significant strength, or a region struck by a period of extended drought, or a flood caused by intense rains in a seasonal strong storm. Hot summers. Cold winters. All these normal weather-related events have happened many times in the history of the planet.

There is no viable scientific evidence of climate crisis, systemic extreme-weather patterns, or any significant loss of the polar ice caps. The UN IPCC's Fifth Assessment Report (AR5) in 2014 delicately repudiated the climate crisis narrative promoted by Al Gore and the climate extremist movement, by stating: 1) *"current datasets indicate no significant observed trends in global tropical cyclone frequency over the past century"*; 2) *"no robust trends in annual numbers of tropical storms, hurricanes and major hurricane counts have been identified over the past 100 years in the north Atlantic basin"*; 3) *"there continues to be a lack of evidence of any trend of increased magnitude or frequency of flood on a global scale"*; 4) *"there is low confidence in detection and attribution of changes in drought over global land areas since the mid-20th century"*.

The facts are the facts. Even the UN IPCC had to admit it. There has been no global increase in systemic extreme-weather patterns.

The "Natural" Global Warming Argument

There are many scientists who argue that "global warming" has existed periodically long before the invention of the internal combustion engine and the "Industrial Revolution" (1820). These scientists note that Earth's climate has been in a constant state of change, dominated by ice ages and glaciers for the past 2.5 billion years, and that the earth is currently enjoying a temporary break from the "deep freeze", as it has before.

This theory states that the recent global warming trend started about 11,000 years ago when the earth was warming out of a time when much of North America, Europe and Asia were buried under massive levels of glacier ice. That glacial period is known as the "Pleistocene Epoch".

The earth is about 4.5 billion years old. Looking through a global historical viewpoint, approximately every 100,000 years the earth's climate warms up "temporarily". These warm periods, called "interglacial periods", appear to last approximately 20,000 years before returning to a cold ice age climate. We are currently at approximately year 11,000 and counting, in the most recent warm period.

Global warming during the Earth's current interglacial warm period has significantly reshaped and enhanced the surface of the planet, and the environment. Since the end of the last glacial period, Earth's temperature has risen approximately 16 degrees Fahrenheit, and sea levels have risen about 300 feet! Forests have returned where once there was only ice. About 15,000 years ago the earth had warmed enough to stop the advance of the glaciers. By about 8,000 years ago the land bridge that previously existed across the Bering Strait (between Alaska and Russia) was covered by the

Pacific Ocean, cutting off the migration of humans and animals from Asia to North America.

During the period of time from approximately 1000 AD to 1350 AD (known as the "Medieval Warm Period"), the global temperature was at or higher than the average global temperature of today. Obviously, there was no industrial activity or internal combustion engines generating CO_2 during that period of time. Then from 1350 AD to about 1800 AD the earth entered the "Little Ice Age" when the global average surface temperature of the earth was about 2.0 degrees Fahrenheit colder than today.

Our modern climate represents a relatively short warm period (in global history perspective) between glacial advances. Small-scale cycles of about 40 years exist within larger-scale cycles of about 400 years, which in turn exist inside much larger scale cycles of 20,000 years. These "40 year" cycles are illustrated in recent history by the cooling period of 1940 to 1970, followed by the warming period of 1975 to 1997 and the subsequent period of no warming for the 20 years through 2016.

The modern activist theory that man-made carbon dioxide emissions are directly responsible for global warming is very clearly dispelled by historical fact. The period in time from 7500 to 4000 years B.P. (before present) known as the "Holocene Maximum" is a great illustration. The Holocene Maximum was the hottest period in human history, and it was clearly before humans created the internal combustion engine.

CO_2 in the atmosphere has been increasing for the last 18,000 years. This was confirmed by an Ice Core drilling from the Soviet Station "Vostok" in Antarctica, in a collaborative ice-drilling project between Russia, the United States, and France. More importantly, the CO_2 concentrations in earth's atmosphere move with temperature, not preceding the temperature growth. Both temperatures and CO_2 have been on the increase for 18,000 years. Furthermore, CO_2 has lagged an average of about 800 years *behind* the temperature changes, indicating that CO_2 is not the primary driver of incremental temperature changes.

The total *man-made carbon dioxide* contribution to the greenhouse gases account for only about 0.28% of the cumulative "greenhouse effect". Approximately 99.72% of the "greenhouse effect" is due to natural causes, mostly water vapor and traces of other gases, which we can do nothing at all about. The UN global warming activist scientists do not agree with this carbon dioxide greenhouse gas effect forcing summary, but then again, their climate model predictions have not been at all accurate.

Conclusion: *Eliminating human activity entirely would have little impact on the climate whatsoever.* But doing so would devastate the human existence.

There have been five ice ages in the last 2.5 billion years of the earth's history. Within the ice ages, there are periods of extensive glacier coverage (known as glacial periods) and warmer climate times that are known as interglacial periods. The earth has managed to start and end four massive ice ages that lasted tens of millions of years each during the last 2.4 billion years, all before there was any human existence on the planet.

There are many natural processes at work both within the earth's climate system, and that are impacting the planet from the solar system, that have caused the warming that ended the prior ice ages. These natural processes are far more powerful than anything that mankind can do. I will discuss these processes for you in a later chapter.

Chapter Three

What Is The Evidence For Global Warming?

The global warming activists focus on the fact that human activities are causing an increase in the concentration of CO_2 in the earth's atmosphere because of the use of fossil fuels. They claim that there is a direct correlation between the higher CO_2 concentration, and the earth's temperature. They further claim that the alleged higher global average surface temperature will cause a variety of bad outcomes in the planet's climate in the future.

As I have stated previously, most of the noise that the global warming activists are making relates to predictions of future events. "Trust me" they say. "The severity of the predictions makes global warming a matter that we must all accept". Not one of their prior climate predictions has ever become reality. In this chapter, I will walk you through the so-called "evidence" of the existence of the alleged man-made global warming, that has been put forth by Al Gore, Barack Obama, and the UN IPCC climate scientists.

CO2 concentration in the atmosphere has increased

As we discussed in chapter two, the current concentration of the carbon dioxide compared to the total greenhouse gases in the atmosphere is 400 "parts per million". While CO_2 is a very small percentage of the atmosphere's greenhouse gas volume (about 10%), the carbon dioxide concentration in the atmosphere in the year 1800 was 280 parts per million, so there has been a 42% increase in the CO_2 concentration in the last 200 years. If you are a part of the group that argues that carbon dioxide is the direct cause of global warming in the recent time, then you might be saying "game over", we have won the argument.

But hold on just a minute. There is a big problem with that, based on the behavior of the global average temperatures in the last 166 years. We know that the earth's global average temperature has warmed by a net total of about 1.5 degrees Fahrenheit since 1850. We also know that about 70% of that increase in global average surface temperature actually occurred before 1940.

In comparison, 75% of the growth in the CO_2 concentration caused by emissions from human activities has occurred after 1940, when only 30% of the temperature rise has happened. Are you seeing the disconnect here? If higher CO_2 concentration in the atmosphere is the direct cause of global warming, then why did 70% of the temperature rise occur before 1940 when we know that CO_2 emissions were much lower. After 1940 the overall temperature rise slowed down, while CO_2 emissions increased significantly. Furthermore, there has been no temperature rise in the last 20 years whatsoever, during which CO_2 emissions have been at the highest levels in human history.

Put simply, you can't "have your cake", and eat it too. If there is a direct correlation between CO_2 emissions and global warming, then there is something missing in that theory. Moreover, it is most likely that any correlation that may exist between CO2 concentration and the earth's temperature variance, is being over-powered by the many counter-acting natural processes occurring within the earth's climate, as well as some very powerful outside forces that are acting on the planet from the solar system. We will discuss these counter-acting natural processes in chapter six.

Earth's temperature has risen 1.5 degrees since 1850

This fact is undisputed by either side of the scientific argument over global warming. There is also no dispute about the pattern of the temperature variances since surface temperatures began to be documented around 1850. During the period from 1850 – 1940, the earth's average temperature warmed by about 1.04 degrees Fahrenheit. Then during the period from 1940 – 1970, the earth's average temperature *cooled* by about <0.36> degrees Fahrenheit. Then, from 1975 – 1997 there was warming of approximately 0.72 degrees Fahrenheit. Since 1997, there has been no change in the earth's average surface temperature, a period of 20 years. It is being called *"the Pause"*, and it is driving the global warming activist scientists and the climate models crazy.

The "Pause" does not fit the global warming science narrative of there being a direct correlation between CO2 concentrations, and warming of the planet's average surface temperature. Not one scientist or any of their climate models predicted the "Pause". The reality is that the 1.5 degree increase in the average surface temperature of the planet in 166 years is not noticeable, and it has not caused harm to the environment. It is a normal climate variation based on the history of the earth.

Stronger & more frequent Hurricanes

Since 1900, the U.S. mainland has averaged two landfalls per year by a hurricane. During the 10-year period of 1996 – 2005 there were a total of 20 hurricanes that made landfall (an average of 2 per year). During the 10-year period from 2006 – 2015 there were only eight hurricanes that made landfall in the U.S. (less than one per year). The 2016 hurricane season saw two hurricanes make landfall on the east coast of the U.S., and both storms were relatively mild category one hurricanes.

The 2005 season was very active with five hurricanes making U.S. mainland landfall. Four of the five storms were rated category three at landfall. The 2005 Atlantic season was the most active Atlantic hurricane season in recorded history, shattering numerous records. Hurricane Katrina attracted unprecedented worldwide attention because of the catastrophic failure of the New Orleans levees and flood walls. Many hysterical claims were made because of the 2005 season, wildly predicting that future hurricanes would be more numerous and more intense, allegedly because of global warming. However, 2005 was a single year extreme season, and as illustrated above by the actual storm data history, the actual hurricane activity has fallen below U.S. historical averages since 2005 (11 consecutive years).

There is no evidence of systematic changes in the magnitude or intensity of extreme meteorological events, such as hurricanes. Highly intense storms can occur randomly, however there is no clear connection to unnatural phenomenon. The facts are simply indisputable. Recall that in chapter two, we discussed that the UN IPCC's Fifth Assessment Report (AR5) released during 2014, disclosed that there has been "*no trends in annual numbers of tropical storms, hurricanes and major hurricane counts over the past 100 years in the north Atlantic basin"*.

Extreme weather – Droughts

Two of the most famous and outspoken proponents of the theory of man-made global warming are Al Gore and Barack Obama, and both have said on many occasions that droughts will become more frequent, and will be of longer duration, due to global warming.

Let's take a look at the facts about drought in the United States. Facts from history, not predictions. During the 19th century, there was an average of one major drought per decade, and the droughts primarily occurred in the west or the southwest part of the United States. Record keeping became more robust in the 20th century. Drought activity was mild from 1900 to 1929, but then came the 1930's. The "dust bowl" drought of 1934 through 1940 was extreme in terms of the duration of the drought and the environmental impact. The areas affected were primarily the panhandles of Oklahoma and Texas but this drought also impacted portions of Colorado, New Mexico, Kansas, and Nebraska. The effects of the drought were made worse by poor farming methods and land management techniques, which resulted in an extensive loss of top soil.

Drought occurrences during the 1940's were relatively mild. The decade of the 1950's saw Texas have a serious drought from 1950-1956. During 1953-1957 there were drought conditions in the Rocky Mountain region and in the Midwest. During 1962-1966 there was an unusual drought in the northeast, when temperatures were mild, but the precipitation was significantly below normal. There was a severe drought in California during 1976-1977.

During 1987-1989 approximately one-third of the United States was in a drought, including the Great Plains, the Midwest, the Northern Plains and the Southeast. There was a particularly large forest fire in Yellowstone during this drought. There was drought in the Southeast during 1993, and then during 1999 drought persisted in much of the Mid-Atlantic States.

During 2002 there was a drought that affected the West, the Rocky Mountain region, and the Midwest. In 2005, there was a wide spread drought that covered Arkansas, Louisiana, Missouri, Iowa, Tennessee, and Illinois. There were significant droughts that affected Texas and California during 2007-2009, and again during 2011-2015.

If you look at the facts you will see a pattern. The pattern is that there is at least one major drought somewhere in the United States every decade. You will also notice that California and Texas are very drought prone.

The geography of Texas will explain why the state is prone to wide spread and extended drought, approximately every other decade. About ten percent of the state is literally a desert, and another twenty percent is dry arid area located between the plains of central Texas and the desert to the west. These areas tend to be hot and dry, even when not in a drought. The government of the State of Texas has planned well, and made infrastructure investments for the frequent drought conditions by building numerous reservoirs throughout the state, to provide for water needs when droughts occur.

California deserves some analysis because it is the most drought prone state in the U.S. mainland. California averages at least one drought every decade, with each drought averaging two to four years in duration. The worst period of drought in California's history was during 1915-1939, notably prior to the substantial increase in CO_2 emissions in the United States. About one-third of California is a desert, and about one-fourth of the state is either arid or semi-arid. So, overall nearly sixty percent of the state of California is very dry terrain. Southern California is completely dependent on the northern part of the state for its water. California droughts are typically ended by a winter season with a pattern of massive storms from the Pacific northwest that bring drenching rains to the northern and central parts of the state, as well as huge snow storms in the Sierra Nevada mountain range. The snow melt in the spring and summer becomes a source of much needed water for the entire state.

Unlike Texas the government of the State of California has done nothing to plan for the very well known risk of frequent and sometimes lengthy droughts, that are a virtual certainty to continue to occur because of the state's geography and climate. The reasons for the lack of badly needed environmental hazard planning includes sustained poor decision making for decades by the state's governors and legislators, environmental activism and litigation, and political activism that shifts the state's critical resources and legislative attention away from the good of the majority of the citizens, toward the political will of a minority with significant political power.

The state of California has not built any new reservoirs since 1979, despite the obvious need for infrastructure to deal with the threat to the state's water resources. California has a freeway system and water resource infrastructure that was built for the needs of about 20 million citizens. The population of the state is now 39 million. There is absolutely no excuse for this irresponsible management by the state's government.

The state and local governments of California are more focused on the politically charged cause of "allowing the proliferation of illegal immigration", allegedly for the needs of agriculture labor, and in the minds of some liberal activists for humanitarian purposes. These governments have neglected the obvious and critical needs of the majority of the legal and tax paying residents. If you live in California, you should be outraged at this neglect.

The bottom line from the analysis of the history of drought in the United States, is that there has been no systematic increase in either the frequency or the magnitude of the regular pattern of drought on the U.S. mainland. Drought is a normal occurrence in certain parts of the nation.

Furthermore, the UN IPCC has reported that there is no evidence of any trend of increase in drought over global land areas since the mid-20th century in their UN IPCC Fifth Assessment Report (AR5), issued in 2014. Droughts continue to occur globally where they normally occur, at the same frequency and duration.

Declining Arctic Sea Ice

The scientists and environmental activists who promote the theory of man-made global warming, make reference to the northern polar ice cap, also known as the Arctic Ocean sea ice. Predictions have been made about the alleged melting of the Arctic sea ice being caused by global warming, and the potential for catastrophic environmental impacts.

Most people know very little about the Arctic Ocean and the Arctic sea ice because it is so geographically remote. So, let's get to know the Arctic Ocean and the sea ice that covers the North Pole. Try to visualize being above the globe, and looking down on the top of the world. First, the North Pole is not located on land. The northern polar cap of the earth, is covered by the Arctic Ocean. The north pole is also covered by floating sea ice, which floats on the surface of the Arctic Ocean. Portions of the ice that does not melt away seasonally is very deep, averaging from 10 to 13 feet thick, with ridges that can build up to 60 feet thick, or more. The Arctic Ocean is surrounded by land masses including Canada, Alaska, Greenland, Norway, and Russia.

The Arctic sea ice covers nearly all the Arctic Ocean during the winter season. The extent is enormous. At the end of the winter when the sea ice reaches its maximum extent, the ice covers an area of approximately 5.8 million square miles. For some perspective, that is the size of the continental United States and the continent of Australia, combined! At the end of the summer season when some of the outer extent of the ice sheet melts away every year, the extent of the ice coverage is about 2.7 million square miles. That is the size of Australia. So, the Arctic sea ice melts by about

50% every summer, and then it refreezes and grows back to its full extent during the late fall and winter.

Wind and ocean currents keep the ice sheet in almost continuous motion on and around the Arctic Ocean, which causes the formation of cracks and sometimes open ponds in the ice, as well as what are called "pressure ridges". The ice can become stacked up in the pressure ridges, and project down under the surface of the ocean to as much as 30 to 80 feet thick. The summer sea ice melt usually occurs between approximately 60 degrees and 75 degrees North latitude. Above 75 degrees North latitude the sea ice remains permanently frozen year round. However, even in that permanent ice sheet, there can be as much as 10 percent of the ice sheet open in various spots, with the ocean surface exposed, because of the cracks and ponds created by the continuous motion of the wind and currents. These cracks and ponds can open and close nearly daily, which can cause opportunity, as well as life threatening risks, for wildlife.

The Arctic Ocean sea ice is prone to some long term and short term variations (also referred to as "high decadal variability") in the level of the seasonal sea ice melt and refreeze extent range. It is known that the Arctic sea ice melted more than usual during the 1920s and 1930s. Then, the Arctic began a long period that lasted through and peaked in 1979, during which the sea ice winter extent continued to expand. Coincidentally, it was in 1979 that NASA first began using new satellites to take images of the polar sea ice. As a result, the 1979 images that are used as the "base line" for comparison to current sea ice levels, were at the maximum extent of the past 100 years.

During the period beginning in 2005 and running through 2012, the Arctic sea ice melted at a higher than normal rate during the summer seasons, and did not fully recover during those years of winter refreeze. As a result, the total extent of the sea ice receded by approximately ten percent, as compared to the 1979 satellite images. This caused a lot of speculation in the scientific community, as well as some hysterical predictions from Al Gore, Barack Obama, and others that the Arctic sea ice was on its way to extinction in the near future. However, the eight-year period of receding sea ice ended dramatically in the winter refreeze season of

2013-2014. The depleted Arctic sea ice re-grew by an area equivalent to the size of Alaska (600,000 square miles) to get back to the extent of the 1979 satellite image. You probably never heard that reported on the evening news.

During the summer of 2014 there were numerous yachts and small ships that made plans to sail the "Northwest Passage" from the Atlantic Ocean to the Pacific Ocean. However, the passage remained clogged with pack ice for the full year, so some boats had to be rescued by ice breakers, while others simply turned around and cancelled their attempt.

The Northwest Passage is a sea route that connects the Atlantic and Pacific Oceans through the Canadian Arctic Archipelago. The potential benefits of the Northwest Passage being clear of sea ice are significant. Shipping routes from Europe to eastern Asia would be 4,000 kilometers (2,500 miles) shorter.

If you have doubts about the health and continued extent of the Arctic sea ice, just consider the facts of the international shipping industry, and the economic benefit that would be provided *"if"* there was a smaller ice pack in the Northwest

Passage. The trip from the Atlantic Ocean to the Pacific Ocean if traversed through the Northwest Passage, would be about three days shorter than sailing south in the Atlantic Ocean to cross via the Panama Canal, to access the Pacific Ocean. The cost savings would be substantial for international shipping companies, and for all the products that are being shipped.

Despite the optimism of the global warming crowd about the sea ice melting during 2005-2012, the Department of Environment and Natural Resources of Canada's Northwest Territories says that "*commercial traffic hasn't increased in the Northwest Passage at all*". The thickness and extent of the Arctic sea ice which can persist throughout the summers indicate what are termed by the Arctic Ocean experts as "*serious ice conditions*". The winds and currents shift the ice constantly, often clogging channels that had been clear the week, or even the day before. The Northwest Passage will be "inhospitable" to international shipping for the reasonably foreseeable future as there is no realistic expectation for a change in the continued extent of the Arctic sea ice.

Finally, the Arctic Ocean with the North Pole and the Arctic sea ice is not a "sensitive environment". It is a robust and harsh environment that is suited to benefit the earth's global climate. It is not an environment that is suitable for human inhabitance. The winter months of December through March see no sunlight, and the temperatures range from -50 degrees, to +10 degrees Fahrenheit. The spring has some sunlight, but the temperatures are still very cold and remain below freezing. During the summer from July through September the temperature can average 32 degrees, and the sun does not set. Finally, in the fall when the sea ice refreeze commences the sun is very low on the horizon, and the temperature falls and stays down around 0 degrees Fahrenheit.

In summary, there just simply is no empirical evidence of a significant warming in the Arctic Ocean at the north pole, or any sustained loss of the Arctic sea ice.

Melting of the Greenland Ice Sheet and Antarctic Ice Cap

Predictions have been made by global warming activists of a substantial melting of the Greenland ice sheet, as well as the Antarctic (south pole) ice cap as a result of alleged global warming.

Greenland is located within the Arctic Circle between Canada and Norway. Greenland is very near to the North Pole of the earth. The Greenland ice sheet is a huge body of ice that covers 660,000 square miles, or roughly 80% of the surface of Greenland. The ice sheet is 1,500 miles long and 680 miles wide. The ice ranges from 1.25 miles (6,600 feet) to 1.9 miles (9,800 feet) in thickness. The aging ice sheet is more than 10,500 feet thick at its highest point. The ice sheet has covered large parts of Greenland for the last 2 to 3 million years. The ice is so heavy that it has depressed the land mass underneath to below sea level. Much of the Greenland ice sheet is surrounded by mountains.

Fewer than 60,000 people live in Greenland because of the cold polar climate. Human occupation is limited to the lower latitudes in the southwest part of the island, which is across the Northwest Passage from far northern Canada. In the capital city of Nuuk, the temperature reaches above freezing (32 degrees Fahrenheit) only 4 months of the year. The average high temperature in July is 46 degrees Fahrenheit.

Eight months of the year it is below freezing, and six months of the year it is brutally cold, with average temperatures ranging between 0 degrees and 20 degrees Fahrenheit. That is in the southern end of the island which is most human habitable. Most of the island covered in ice is much colder, and is uninhabitable. The Greenland ice sheet is not a delicate or sensitive environment.

Antarctica is located on the earth's southern polar cap, at the "bottom of the world". Antarctica is an even more extreme cold environment than the north pole. About 98% of Antarctica is covered by the Antarctic ice sheet, a massive sheet of ice averaging at least 1.0 mile thick. The mean annual temperature of the interior of Antarctica is 57 degrees *below 0* Celsius (70.6 degrees *below 0* Fahrenheit). The coast is "warmer", though even there the summer season temperature is below 0 degrees Celsius (32 degrees Fahrenheit) most of the time. This is cold beyond your ability to imagine it. Antarctica has been covered by ice for the last 15 million years.

Antarctica covers 5.4 million square miles, which is almost twice the size of the U.S. mainland. Antarctica is inhabited only by scientists on research projects. No-one lives in Antarctica indefinitely in the way that people do in the rest of the world, because it is so extremely cold year-round. It has no commercial industries, no towns or cities, no permanent residents. Antarctica is different from the Arctic polar region, because Antarctica is a land mass and most of the southern polar ice sits on top of the land, while the Arctic (north pole) ice is primarily floating atop the Arctic Ocean (except for the Greenland ice sheet). So, the Antarctic ice field does not grow and shrink with the seasons like the Arctic ice field does. In fact, despite all the global warming hysteria, the Antarctic ice field is actually growing. That's right, it is growing.

According to calculations in the UN IPCC's 2007 report, in the next 100 years Greenland and Antarctica combined will add a little over 6 centimeters (2.5 inches) to sea level, meaning there will not be any sudden collapse of fresh water or a sudden rise in global sea levels. Again, there is no empirical evidence of any significant warming in the Arctic Ocean (Greenland) or any loss of the Antarctic ice sheet (the south pole).

The hottest years on record have occurred "since 2000"

NASA and NOAA have issued press releases claiming the three hottest years on record for global average surface temperatures have been in the three consecutive years of 2014, 2015 and 2016.

The New York Times published an article on January 18, 2017 with the headline "Earth Sets a Temperature Record for the Third Straight Year". The article is accompanied with a lovely color photograph of some very sparse sea ice in the midst of open ocean. The article opens under the photo with, "*Marking another milestone for a changing planet, scientists reported on Wednesday that the Earth reached its highest temperature on record in 2016, trouncing a record set only a year earlier, which beat one set in 2014. It is the first time in the modern era of global warming data that temperatures have blown past the previous record three years in a row*".

Oh!... and then next the article states "*The findings come two days before the inauguration of an American president who has called global warming a Chinese plot and vowed to roll back his predecessor's efforts to cut emissions of heat-*

trapping gases". OK – no political bias on display there, right?

The NY Times article does not give the actual global average surface temperatures in the years referenced for comparison, but it does admit that "*2016 set a record by only a small amount*". It turns out that 2016 exceeded 2015 by 0.018 Fahrenheit (less than two-one hundredths of one degree). At that rate, it would take 55 years to go up by one degree. It is equivalent to a broadcaster for a football game on television saying, "the gain on first and ten was just two-one hundredths of a yard, so, now it is second and ten". And oh, by the way, both 2015 and 2016 were "El Nino" years when there is a normal, natural rise in temperatures.

Again, as stated previously there has been no empirical evidence of any real warming of the global average surface temperature of the earth since 1997.

Retreating Glaciers worldwide

During the last 25,000 years, glaciers around the world have fluctuated widely in concert with changes in the climate, sometimes shrinking to extents and volumes smaller than today. Mountain glaciers around the world display a wide variety of responses to local climate variation, and have not responded to global temperature change in a simple, uniform way.

Tropical mountain glaciers in both South America and Africa (below the equator) have retreated in the last 100 years because of reduced precipitation and increased solar radiation. Some glaciers elsewhere also have retreated since the end of the Little Ice Age (1850). Many glaciers retreated aggressively during the 1915–1940 period of surface temperature warming, which was prior to significant industrial CO_2 emissions. These same glaciers advanced during the 1940–1975 period of cooling when human CO_2 emissions were growing even faster. This is the opposite reaction of what would have happened if human-caused CO_2 emissions were the direct cause of increased warming *and* melting of glaciers.

There is a limited amount of quantitative observations of mountain glaciers prior to 1860, however inferences can be made about earlier advances and retreats from paintings, sketches, and historical documents. Fossil wood, tree stumps, human artifacts, and dwellings indicate that in earlier historic times glaciers in the European Alps were smaller than today, and situated farther up in their valleys.

During the last millennium, glaciers have advanced and retreated multiple times as the Earth has passed through the Medieval Warm Period, the Little Ice Age, and the warming of the twentieth century. For most of the glaciers that have retreated during the twentieth century, shrinkage generally started in the late nineteenth century, many decades before the significant growth in human caused CO_2 emissions, after World War II would have been a factor.

No unprecedented warming has occurred in the twentieth century (+1.5 degrees global average temp in 166 years). Glaciers have retreated during the 1915–1940 period of warming before there was major industrial CO_2 emissions, and advanced during the 1940–1975 cooling period when CO_2 emissions were growing even faster, not indicative of CO_2 as the direct cause of the warming and glacial melting.

No substantive evidence exists that the rate of glacier retreat has increased over the last 50 years, a time of large increases in CO2 emissions. Moreover, it is a normal process for glaciers to retreat during interglacial periods, which the planet has been in for about 11,000 years.

Rising Sea Levels

Sea-level rise is one of the most feared environmental impacts of the discussion of possible future global warming, for the global warming activists. Wild and hysterical predictions and illustrations of catastrophic coastal flooding and the literal loss of major U.S. cities to ocean water inundation have been produced by some of the more allegorical man-made global warming advocates.

There is a wide variance between the actual amount of sea level rise observed in recent history, and the magnitude of sea level rise that is being predicted by various global warming activists and climatologists who frequently project the effects of the alleged increase in man-made global warming.

The observed rate of actual sea-level rise that has been documented during the recent century (1900-1999) is an average of approximately 1.8 mm per year. If you are not fluent in the metric system, there are 25.4 mm (millimeters) in one inch, so at 1.8 mm per year it would take 14 years for the sea level to rise by one inch. This is actual sea level rise data, and it is not in dispute.

Sea level has been tracked around the world for about 200 years. This has been done with tide gauges, which are water-level recorders anchored to some fixed structure along the coastline, maybe a wharf, a concrete breakwater or some other solid structure that is stable over long periods of time. The oldest tide gauge in the world is on the coast of Poland and was installed in 1808. In the United States, there are tide gauges that have been in operation since 1856, in various locations on the east coast and on the west coast. There are many other newer tide gauges that have been installed in the past 50-75 years.

Satellite measurements of sea level made by radar ranging altimetry have been available only since the early 1990s. Until recently, these satellite measurements indicated a rate of global sea-level rise of approximately 3.2 mm per year, nearly twice the rate measured by tide gauges over the last century. That information was like gasoline on a fire for the global warming activists. Over the past few years, however, the satellite-measured rate of sea level rise has been closer to 2 mm per year, a measure much closer to the tide gauge measurements recorded for the last century.

Sea level variability is a known factor in tracking sea levels. Short-term and medium-term sea-levels vary significantly on decadal and multidecadal time scales with regard to a "60-year-long oceanographic cycle". There is a significant oscillation (regular variation) with a period of around 60-years in the majority of the tide gauges examined during the 20th Century and it appears in every ocean basin. This known oscillation basically negates any sea level data analysis that is done for a period of time shorter than 60 years.

This casts great doubt on the reliability of the Satellite measurements that indicated a rate of global sea-level rise of approximately 3.2 mm per year, during only the 1990s-decade time frame, as we then saw that the satellite-measured rate of sea level rise has been closer to 2 mm per year recently, following the known factor of oscillation. In other words, you can't take the 3.2 mm/year rate of sea level rise found in a single decade, and project out into the long term future based only on that single decadal measurement. It is a factually false assumption.

When the sea level data is viewed in the proper perspective with regard to time *there is no empirical evidence indicating that sea level rise is accelerating* beyond the average experienced in the last century. Furthermore, there is no evidence of a significant acceleration of polar ice cap melting to impact the recent century historical trend.

As a side note on this subject, particularly for the attention of Al Gore, the temporary storm surge that is created by a hurricane making landfall on the mainland is not indicative of sea level rise. You wouldn't think that you would need to state the obvious, but in the case of Al Gore, it is necessary.

Global warming made Donald J. Trump win the election

It wasn't the Russians. CNN, MSNBC, NBC, ABC, CBS, and every other liberal rag has gotten this wrong. I am the first analyst to get this right. Nearly every national poll predicted that Hillary Clinton would win the Presidential election over Donald Trump in November 2016. Before the last 60 days of the campaign Hillary Clinton's lead in the polls was substantial, and the network pundits routinely proclaimed that Hillary had a 90% chance of winning the election, as they scoffed at Trump's massive campaign rallies. Nearer to election day, polls were showing a sustained but narrowing lead for Hillary Clinton. The last five polls published on "RealClearPolitics" showed Hillary leading Trump by three percentage points (within the "margin of error").

So, what in the world happened? A real estate tycoon and reality TV star with no political experience, first wins the Republican nomination by defeating a field of 17 highly qualified Presidential candidates made up of senators, governors, physicians and CEOs. Then, this political novice runs a unique Presidential campaign against the "smartest woman in the world", whom President Barack Obama defined with this amazing statement: *"I can say with confidence there has never been a man or a woman—not me, not Bill, nobody—more qualified than Hillary Clinton to serve as president of the United States of America"*. Now that's an endorsement! And from the sitting President, no less. Game over!

Well then, that settles it! There is only one way to explain former Secretary of State Hillary Clinton losing the election to Donald J. Trump. Global Warming. -- Global Warming!! It was global warming that caused all those voters to lose their minds and push the wrong button, in all of those important swing states on election day.

It couldn't have been because Hillary Clinton had set up a private, unsecure (and unauthorized) email server to handle all of her emails as the Secretary of State; or that she knowingly sent or received classified material on her unsecured email system, and most likely harmed national security by doing so; or that she had been misleading or completely dishonest about a number of claims she made to defend herself; or that FBI director James Comey found that Hillary and her staff had been "*extremely careless*" in the handling of highly sensitive information and that it was "*possible that hostile actors gained access to Secretary Clinton's personal e-mail account*". Nah, that's not it.

It couldn't have been because The State Department, under Secretary Clinton, significantly reduced the security detail at the Benghazi consulate facility at a time of civil war in the streets; *and,* then denied Ambassador Stevens' July 2012 request for 13 additional American security personnel; *and,* then after the brutal murders of Ambassador Stevens, a State Department Information Officer and two CIA Officers (both former Navy Seals), Secretary Clinton carried on the false narrative that the attack in Benghazi was because of an anti-Muslim video, when her own emails revealed that Clinton knew almost immediately that it was an orchestrated assault. *And,* certainly it can't be because during Secretary Clinton's testimony in front of the U.S. House Oversight Committee in May 2013 about the events of September 11, 2012 in Benghazi, Secretary Clinton responded to a question about the facts of the terror attack, and the subsequent communications by the State Department with, "'*What difference, at this point, does it make?*'". Right, the four Americans are still dead. Nah, that's not it.

It couldn't have been because during a campaign speech at the "LGBT for Hillary" Gala in New York City on September 9, 2016, Hillary said, "*You know, to just be grossly generalistic, you could put half of Trump's supporters into what I call the* **basket of deplorables**. *Right? The racist,* *sexist, homophobic, xenophobic, Islamaphobic -- you name it"*. Hillary basically threw about 30 million voters (if not more), some of whom may have been undecided, into the Trump bucket. But nah, that's not it.

It couldn't have been because during the time that Hillary was serving as The Secretary of State, the Clinton Foundation was able to collect donations in excess of $150 million from foreign governments, foreign dignitaries and individuals. Nah, that's not it.

It couldn't have been because she didn't have any ability to connect with the voters; or that she is arrogant, entitled and self-absorbed; or that she had no real campaign message other than "*I am a woman*", and "*Donald Trump is not fit to be President*". Nah, that's not it either.

Or maybe, the voters just bought into the whole "Make America Great Again" campaign brand of Donald J. Trump; the huge rallies where crowds of 10,000 to 20,000 (depending on the venue size) were routinely showing up to see Trump; the "build the wall" immigration policy; the "America first" trade policy; Tax cuts/reform and economic growth; strong foreign policy; repeal Obamacare, and "drain the swamp"! Nah, that's not it.

In the 2016 Presidential election candidate Donald J. Trump: (1) won 30 states; (2) won 304 electoral college votes (57%) to 227 for Hillary; and (3) carried 2,623 out of 3,112 counties (84%). In the end, as an electoral outcome it wasn't even close!

So, Hillary won the total popular vote by 2.9 million votes (2% of the total). *However*, the founding fathers of the nation had the foresight to design the electoral college to make every state's vote for the White House count proportionally and strategically.

You see, Hillary's popular vote margin came from just two very blue and out of touch states...New York +1.7 million votes; and California +4.2 million votes.

It was that darned Global Warming! *(tongue planted firmly in cheek)*

Chapter Four

Global Warming Predictions

Reality. The word is defined by Webster's Dictionary as: (1) the quality or state of being real; (2) a real event, entity, or state of affairs; (3) the totality of real things and events.

If you look up the meaning of "Reality" on the search engine "*Google*", you get: (1) the world or the state of things as they actually exist as opposed to an idealistic or notional idea of them; (2) the state or quality of having existence or substance.

When you look up "Reality" in the thesaurus, you get these results: "existence, real world, realism, truth, actuality, authenticity, certainty, genuineness, realness, substance, validity"...and there is even more. I prefer the Google definition – "*the world or the state of things as they actually exist, as opposed to an idealistic or notional idea of them*".

Global warming...Climate Change. Unless you are living under a rock, you have at least heard of it, and you have most likely heard of it from someone that is prominent in today's "pop culture". Many pop culture icons have been, and continue to be very outspoken about the issue of global warming. They tend to use their very public platforms to try to shape public opinion. They also tend to attempt to repeat the global warming narrative in ways that make it obvious that they really don't know much about what they are talking about.

How are members of pop culture qualified to educate you on the issue of global warming? Are they scientists? Have they studied the facts, the history, the statistics and the "*Reality*" of global warming on the planet? Many of the members of pop culture are making bold and scary claims and catastrophic predictions about the effects of alleged global warming, about what is causing it, and about what should be done to "prevent" it from happening. These pop culture icons and other celebrities are making big demands about things that *you should do* to change how *you live your life*. The best way to judge how much they really know is to look at what they have predicted.

So, let's take a look at what is being said about global warming, who is saying it, and what actual evidence there is to compare to what is being said. Doesn't that sound like a reasonable thing to do, before you interrupt how *you are living your life*?

There are some people who believe that global warming is being caused mostly by human activities, which is the use of fossil fuels (oil, gas, coal). This would include everyday activities such as driving your car, riding a train or an airplane, using electricity or heating oil in your home or office, and the manufacturing activities to make all the products that you use or consume in your daily life. In the alternative, there are some people who believe that global warming is primarily caused by natural processes in the earth's atmosphere and climate systems, that are exclusive from and unrelated to human activities.

For decades we have heard some famous and outspoken people who have bought in to the man-made global warming hoax, using their platform of fame to predict the so-called "tipping point", and to tell us how we should change our lives to stop the alleged global warming. Following are some examples of why you should never let actors or pop culture characters give you any kind of advice.

Brad Pitt – Actor and Producer

During an appearance on "The Daily Show" on the Comedy Central network, Brad Pitt condemned automobiles: Pitt said, *"like, if we invented the automobile today, would we invent a car, would we say, I know!...We'll run it on a finite fossil fuel. We'll export a half a trillion dollars of our GDP. We'll spend hundreds of billions of dollars on our military to protect that interest, and it will pollute the environment! You know, it just doesn't make sense."*

Facts:

First of all did Brad mean to say "import" half a trillion dollars of our GDP? (importing fossil fuels) Oh well, it doesn't matter, he's a movie star so he's awesome. So, let's move on. The automobile was invented around 1885. The internal combustion engine and the automobile as we know it resulted from the discovery of oil in 1847. The development of the affordable automobile has been one of the greatest economic liberators for the average American citizen, promoting access to greater employment and earnings opportunities.

The annual income of the average American worker nearly doubled (from $10,000 to $17,000 per year) within 20 years of the mass production of the American automobile. Today the average income of American workers is seven times what it was before the invention of affordable automobiles (approximately $72,000 per year). Automobiles are more fuel efficient now than ever, and the automobile industry is developing and improving technologies to become even more fuel efficient. The automobile is a critical and indispensable tool in the American economy. Many Americans actually use their automobile to drive to beautiful air-conditioned theaters where they pay to see Brad Pitt's movies. Until we can somehow perfect solar or hydrogen power, or something else yet unseen, the internal combustion engine is the driving force of commerce.

To his credit, Brad Pitt has owned an electric car...a $102,000 Tesla, but do you know how electric cars recharge their batteries? They get plugged in to an electrical outlet which gets the electricity from a big power plant that is fueled by burning coal or natural gas. You see, there is no escaping the fact that about 87% of the energy used in the world today is generated from fossil fuels. That is just the way that it is, because alternative sources of energy as they exist today do not produce a scalable and sufficient supply of dependable and transportable energy at an affordable cost. And by the way Brad, carbon dioxide is not "pollution". You exhale carbon dioxide when you breathe.

Brad Pitt is a frequent user of private jets, which burn about 400 gallons of jet fuel per hour, or more, depending on the size of the jet. So, having Brad Pitt lecture the rest of us about the sins of using automobiles is akin to living in a glass house, and throwing rocks at the neighbors. It's just dumb.

But wait everybody I have some really good news for Brad. The shale genie is out of the bottle. Because of innovations in horizontal drilling, hydraulic fracturing, seismology and other information technology developments, the United States is now at the top of the energy producing nations in the world! The U.S. has more oil than Saudi Arabia and more natural gas than Russia. Supply is plentiful and prices are low.

So, go ahead and charge up that Tesla Brad, and fly around in your private jet. It's not a problem. And you are an awesome actor so everything is just great! But the next time some talk show host tries to suck you in with a lame question about global warming, just tell him that subject is not your specialty. That way you won't sound entitled or stupid. And for the record, my favorite Brad Pitt movies are Moneyball, Fury and Inglorious Basterds`. Oh, and he was good in The Big Short too. Don't be mad at me Brad, I'm a big fan buddy!

George Clooney – Actor, Filmmaker and Activist

Speaking to the press at the BAFTA Awards event in 2013, George Clooney said, *"in the wake of one of the most violent typhoons ever recorded, those who claim humans have nothing to do with causing stronger storms are defending a "stupid and ridiculous" argument. Well, it's just a stupid argument. If you have 99 percent of doctors who tell you 'you are sick', and one percent that says 'yeah you're fine', you'd probably want to check it up for the 99. The idea that we ignore that we are someway involved in climate change is ridiculous".*

Facts:

The leader of the global warming movement is generally accepted to be Al Gore, who has written numerous books and articles on global warming, and produced a well-known documentary film titled "An Inconvenient Truth" that was released in 2006. One of Mr. Gore's stated beliefs is that the rise in CO_2 in the atmosphere will cause an increase in the severity and frequency of certain weather events, such as typhoons. This is what George Clooney appears to be referencing in his comments.

Despite Mr. Clooney's anecdotal opinion, there is no evidence of any observed trend of an increase in the frequency or strength of global occurrences of cyclones or typhoons during the past century. There is also no trend in the increase above normal historical occurrences of tropical storms or hurricanes during the last century in the United

States. That fact was disclosed by the UN IPCC in their "Fifth Assessment Report" issued in 2014.

The United States has averaged two landfalls per year by a hurricane since 1900. During the decade of 1996-2005 there were 20 hurricanes that made landfall on the U.S. mainland, an average of two per year. During the decade of 2006-2015 there were only eight hurricanes that made landfall on the U.S. mainland, an average of less than one per year.

There is no evidence of systematic changes in rainfall, or in the magnitude or intensity of extreme meteorological events, such as typhoons or hurricanes. The difference between the opinions expressed by Al Gore, and hysterically repeated by George Clooney is "systematic" (methodical; repeated; with regularity), rather than "anecdotal" (unscientific observa-tions; a storm or storms, here or there; not repetitive). It is not valid to refer to a single storm, or a single year of storms, and extrapolate that limited sample over a long-term prediction of future events. There is no relationship between storm activity and CO_2 emissions.

Mr. Clooney's reference to the "*99 percent of doctors who tell you 'you are sick', and one percent that says 'yeah you're fine'*", is likely a veiled reference to the assertion that is often made by many global warming activists that "97 percent of scientists allegedly agree that human caused global warming is real". That assertion has been revealed to be a large exaggeration of the facts. It is a reference to a 2013 study by John Cook, an Australian researcher.

Here are the facts of that study. Mr. Cook analyzed abstracts of 11,944 peer-reviewed papers on global warming published between 1991 and 2011, to see what position they took on human influence on the climate. 7,930 of the papers (66%) took no position on man-made global warming at all. 3,896 of the papers (33%) agreed that there is man-made global warming. Mr. Cook concluded that of the papers taking a position on global warming, either explicitly or implicitly, 97% had agreed that humans to some degree contribute to global warming. Mr. Cook extrapolated from a limited sample (33%) of the total population of the papers. The 97% consensus is really the 33% consensus, when the entire population of papers is included. The whole "97% consensus" claim is a flim-flam.

In the world of science "consensus" is not proof of anything. Real scientists know that. As a practical matter, experts can all agree on anything but that doesn't make them right. The vast majority of the pollsters, predicted that Hillary Clinton would win the 2016 Presidential election. But on November 8, 2016 the so-called experts were proven wrong. Donald J. Trump won the election in an electoral college land slide. George Clooney is not stupid, and he is not ridiculous. He is just getting his facts from a very misguided and biased source.

Harrison Ford – Actor and Film Producer

In an interview by an Australian reporter, Harrison Ford was asked what he thought would be the consequences if world leaders were unable to reach an agreement for a plan at the "Paris climate talks" (a UN sponsored meeting of 195 Nations, in November 2015). Harrison Ford's response was: *"Nature will take care of itself...if people knew the benefits of nature besides cute animals and a place for them to vacation, then they would understand the value of nature:*

clean air, fresh water, pollinators for our crops, new medicines, new food crops, that nature provides".

Mr. Ford continued with his response: "*If only people knew that, they'd accept climate alarmism as fact and fight against global warming. If we don't work together to combat climate change, the planet will be ok, there just won't be any damn people on it*".

Facts:

Work together? Really? Harrison Ford owns numerous aircraft and is a private pilot. One of his aircraft is a private jet which he uses to travel to and from his ranch in Wyoming. The jet burns 300-400 gallons of fuel per hour of flight. In an interview in 2010, Ford said that he is passionate about flying and that he often would "*fly up the coast for a cheese burger*". His actions appear to be in conflict with his stated opinion about global warming and what should be done about it. Either he doesn't really believe it, or he just doesn't care. Or, it is your problem, and not his?

Mr. Ford says "*If only people knew the benefits of nature besides cute animals and a place for them to vacation, then they would understand the value of nature, they'd accept climate alarmism as fact and fight against global warming".*

That is a very arrogant and invalid reason for people to "accept climate alarmism as fact". What, we are supposed to accept "climate alarmism" as fact, just because Harrison Ford said it? He gave no substantiation, or valid example, for his opinion. He just gave his opinion.

Hollywood actors with lots of money live a lavish life style and why shouldn't they? If you had Harrison Ford's money, wouldn't you want to live like him? I know that I sure-as-heck would! So, let me be the first to say to Mr. Ford, "I am a big fan of your many movies. Let the global warming guilt trip go my friend. It's not your fault". Or mine. There is no climate crisis. And maybe you should spend more time worrying about which runway, or taxiway (oops), that you are landing your plane on sir. I'm just sayin'.

Barbara Streisand – Singer, songwriter, actress, filmmaker

Speaking to Diane Sawyer of ABC News in September 2005, Barbara Streisand said, *"we are in a global warming emergency state and these storms are going to become more frequent, more intense".* The "Babs" was making reference to Hurricane Katrina (August 2005). She went on to say further, *"there could be more droughts, dust bowls. You know it's amazing to hear these facts, I mean, the Andes have no ice caps on the mountains in winter. The glaciers are melting."*

Facts:

Well clearly Barbara Streisand has watched "An Inconvenient Truth". Unfortunately, she was completely wrong in her prediction about "storms becoming more frequent and more intense". She's not the first. Since 1900, the U.S. mainland has averaged two landfalls per year by a hurricane. During the 10-year period of 1996 – 2005 there were 20 hurricanes that made landfall (an average of two per year). During the 10-year period from 2006 – 2015 there were only eight hurricanes that made landfall in the U.S. (less than one per year). The 2016 hurricane season saw two hurricanes make landfall on the east coast of the U.S., and both storms were relatively mild category one hurricanes.

The 2005 Atlantic hurricane season was the most active Atlantic hurricane season in recorded history, shattering numerous records. Hurricane Katrina attracted unprecedented worldwide attention because of the catastrophic failure of the New Orleans levees and flood walls. Katrina is the poster-child storm for environmental activists to refer to as the worst case, and as an indicator of future calamity because of alleged global warming.

As mentioned previously, scientists have produced studies that show that there is no evidence of systematic changes in the magnitude or intensity of extreme meteorological events, such as typhoons or hurricanes. Highly intense storms or even storm seasons can occur randomly, however there is no pattern of repeat. Point of fact, the hurricane activity in the U.S. has been below average since 2005. Again, the UN IPCC confirmed in their 2014 "Fifth Assessment Report" that there has been no trend of increase of tropical storms or hurricanes over the past 100 years. Sorry Babs.

If Babs would do a little reading on the subject instead of just depending on An Inconvenient Truth, she would find out that it is a normal cyclical pattern for glaciers to retreat (melt) during an interglacial period, which the planet is currently in. Furthermore, there has been no systematic increase in the normal occurrence or duration of droughts in the world. Those areas that are drought prone are experiencing drought conditions, but no more than normal.

John Travolta – Actor and Producer

While responding to the press at an appearance where he was promoting one of his movies, John Travolta said, *"global warming is a very valid issue. Everyone can do their bit. But I don't know if it's not too late already. We have to think about alternative methods of fuel."*

Travolta then said, *"I'm probably not the best candidate to ask about global warming because I fly jets. I use them as a business tool, as others do."*

Facts:

Indeed Mr. Travolta does fly jets. He owns not one, but five jets. One of the jets is a four engine Boeing 707, which when configured for commercial passenger use can seat as many as 200 people. Travolta has a private airstrip that actually connects to his home. He also owns three Gulfstream and one Learjet. Good for him!

As I previously said to Harrison Ford, let me also say to John Travolta: "let the global warming guilt trip go my friend. It's not your fault". Or mine either. There is no climate crisis. As for Mr. Travolta's suggestion that *"We have to think about alternative methods of fuel",* I suggest that John should read chapter six of this book. It has a great ending! And one more thing: I thought John Travolta was very good in "Get Shorty".

Bono (stage name) – lead singer for "U2"

Bono made an appearance with Al Gore at the World Economic Forum in Davos Switzerland in January 2008 to discuss issues of global warming and world poverty. Bono told the gathered press that his career in rock music was not always conducive to a green lifestyle, and he compared a conversation with Al Gore to an act of religious contrition. Bono said, *"it's like being with an Irish priest. You start to confess your sins…Father Al, I am not just a noise polluter, I am a noise-polluting, diesel soaking, gulfstream flying rock star…I'm going to kick the habit. I'm trying Father Al, but oil has been very good for me."*

Al Gore then spoke and said that the world climate crisis was worsening, and was in fact unfolding more rapidly than some of the most pessimistic projections by the Intergovernmental Panel on Climate Change (IPCC).

Bono then said, *"the planet is in a precarious place right now and extreme poverty affects a billion people who are living on less than a dollar a day"*. He then stressed the interconnectedness of the issues of climate change and third world debt relief. He said that the environmental and economic consequences of global warming will only exacerbate efforts to reduce poverty.

Facts:

There are climate cycles that occur naturally. During recent history, there have been three such climate change cycles that are documented by the global average surface temperature. From 1940 to 1970 there was a period of global cooling that resulted in an overall decrease in the global average surface temperature of 0.2 degrees Celsius (which is 0.36 degrees Fahrenheit). You read that right…there was cooling, not warming during 1940-1970, at a time when CO_2 emissions were growing worldwide.

From 1975 to 1997 there was a period of global warming that resulted in an overall increase in the global average surface temperature of 0.4 degrees Celsius (which is 0.72 degrees Fahrenheit).

From 1997 to 2017 there has been no observed change in the global average surface temperature. The global average surface temperature has been flat for the last 20 years, while global CO_2 emissions have continued to grow as more world economies become industrialized. Therefore, there is no evidence of any climate crisis based on the global average surface temperature. That fact is not in dispute.

And by the way with regard to Bono's reference to world poverty, there are still about 1.6 billion people in the world today with no access to electricity. Can you imagine living without electricity? Denying those impoverished human-beings the opportunity to raise their standard of living, is absolutely immoral. Until new energy technologies that do not exist today can be developed, carbon based fuels must continue to provide the energy that mankind needs to survive, and to thrive. The so-called climate crisis exists only in the computer climate models of the UN scientists.

Leonardo DiCaprio – Actor and Film Producer

Leo DiCaprio has become one of the most outspoken environmentalists from the Hollywood elite. He founded the Leonardo DiCaprio Foundation which promotes fund raising and publicity for environmental causes, and he was named a Messenger of Peace by the UN in 2014.

Mr. DiCaprio gave a speech to the UN assembly in New York on Earth Day in 2016. He told the UN assembly and members of the press in attendance, that *"climate change is the defining crisis of our time"*…and *"our planet cannot be saved unless we leave fossil fuels in the ground where they belong"*. Addressing the UN members directly, he said *"You are the last, best hope of Earth. We ask you to protect it, or we and all living things we cherish, are history"*.

On the LDF web site, one of the policy statements reads: "After centuries of exponential population growth and the creation of unsustainable industrial development models driven by dirty, carbon intensive fuels, we have radically altered not just the face of the planet but our climate". It also states, "many scientists believe that we have just five years to reverse the trend of rapidly increasing pollution". Finally, in a statement notably preceded by the word "IF", "If we do not change our course, we could soon be on an irreversible path towards severe climate instability, resource scarcity and environmental degradation, resulting in a planet no longer capable of sustaining life as we currently know it".

Facts:

DiCaprio's claim of a climate "crisis" is not supported by any facts, or demonstrated by any systematic evidence. Leo follows the model of Al Gore, claiming that random extreme weather events are resulting from man-made CO_2 emissions. The fact is that there has been mild warming in the last 150+ years overall of about 1.5 degrees Fahrenheit, and in fact there has been no global warming at all since 1997 (20 years). Stating on the web site that "many scientists believe that we have just five years to reverse the trend of rapidly increasing pollution" is baseless, and is an extremist ploy that has failed repeatedly and embarrassed numerous environmentalists in the last 50 years of the environmental activist movement.

If somehow the UN member nations were to "leave fossil fuels in the ground where they belong" as Mr. DiCaprio stated in his UN speech, then the movie industry in which he makes his fabulous living would not be able to exist, as anyone familiar with the infrastructure and resources necessary to produce major motion pictures, knows all too well. And then there is the frequent use of private jets which burn 300 to 400 gallons of jet fuel per hour, which DiCaprio is well known to use quite often. Can you say "hypocrisy"?

As for the UN being "the last best hope of earth", as DiCaprio put it in his UN speech, well the UN talks a big story, but they don't do much. The Paris Agreement was reached by 171 member nations. Under the agreement the countries set their own targets for reducing emissions of carbon dioxide and other greenhouse gases. The targets are not legally binding, but the countries must "update them" every five years. So, what does that tell you about how serious the UN Assembly is about the alleged "climate crisis"? They all like to tell each other (and you) what to do, but none of the member nations are actually willing to make any material changes themselves. Could that be because they know that "man-made" global warming is really a false narrative, and that all of this bluster is just feel good political rhetoric? Hmm? Or even worse, it is really a hoax to get control of more tax payer money. And Leo DiCaprio is a willing participant in the hoax.

President Barack Obama 44th President of the United States

President Obama has stated that *"there is no greater threat to the future than climate change"*. And, that *"since 1880, the Earth's average surface temperature has warmed by about 1.4 degrees Fahrenheit"*.

The President has also said *"if we do not act forcefully, we'll continue to see rising oceans, longer hotter heat waves, dangerous droughts, and floods"*.

Of course, President Obama also said: *"if you like your health plan, you can keep your health plan"*; *"if you like your doctor, you can keep your doctor"*; *"we will lower health insurance premiums up to $2,500 per year for a typical family"*. Oh, I can't leave this out, Obama also said *"I can say with confidence there has never been a man or a woman, not me not Bill, nobody more qualified than Hillary*

Clinton to serve as President of the United States of America". We know where all of that went. But, I digress.

Facts:

I think that it is safe to say that the United States faces a greater threat to the future from radical Islamic terrorism, ISIS and Al Qaeda, and nuclear weapons in rogue states (N Korea and Iran), than from any alleged global warming or climate variability.

A common sense view of the climate change variability since 1880 suggests that the climate change observed is being caused primarily by natural processes of the earth and the sun, and not in correlation to human emissions of CO_2. The logic is well chronicled: from 1880-1940 there was warming of approximately 1.04 degrees Fahrenheit; from 1940-1970 there was cooling of <0.36> degrees Fahrenheit; from 1975-1997 there was warming of 0.72 degrees Fahrenheit. Since 1997, there has been no temperature variability (the global average temperature has remained flat). This temperature variability history shows that the highest period of warming (1880-1940) was during the lowest period of CO_2 emissions, and that there has been no warming at all during the period of the highest volume of CO2 emissions (1997-2016). This is certainly not what you would expect to see, if in fact CO2 emissions were the sole and direct cause of temperature warming for the planet.

Notwithstanding President Obama's opinion above, no convincing exclusive relationship has been established between warming, CO2 emission volumes, and extreme weather events. Reference the pattern of hurricanes making landfall in the U.S. previously discussed (see Barbara Streisand). President Obama's views are those of a radical ideologue. That doesn't make him a bad guy, but it does make him dangerous, and the end of his term in office (with all due respect) could not have come soon enough.

Meryl Streep – Actress

In 1990 while hosting the PBS series titled "Race to Save the Planet", Meryl Streep stated, *"by the year 2000 the Earth's climate will be warmer than it's been in over 100,000 years. If we don't do something there will be enormous calamities in a very short time"*.

Facts:

The 100,000 year range is completely out of context because it reaches back into glacial periods of the ice age. But Meryl Streep is not a scientist, or apparently a historian either, so we will give her a pass there. The generally characterized "enormous calamities" have not happened in the 27 years since she made her prediction. Furthermore, there has been no warming of the global average temperature since 1997. Meryl Streep and PBS got that one wrong. But they have joined a large and distinguished group of celebrities and dignitaries who have repeatedly gotten their predictions humorously wrong, so they won't be lonely. Liberals are really good at playing "follow the liberal leader" and they are also very easy to spot.

Al Gore – American Politician and Environmentalist

Al Gore has long been at the forefront of the global warming movement, and he was instrumental in bringing the issue to prominence in the current day pop culture. Mr. Gore has written numerous environmental books and produced the screenplay for the environmental documentary "An Inconvenient Truth". He practically single handedly brain washed the Hollywood liberal elites.

While promoting "An Inconvenient Truth" in January 2006, Al Gore stated, *"unless we take drastic measures to reduce greenhouse gases, the world will reach a point of no return in a mere ten years"*. He called it a *"true planetary crisis"*.

Al Gore predicted in "An Inconvenient Truth" that the melting of the Arctic Ocean sea ice and the Greenland glaciers would cause catastrophic sea level rise that would result in the flooding of Miami, New York City, and San Francisco, as well as major coastal cities in Europe and Asia.

Gore also predicted in "An Inconvenient Truth" that the melting of the Arctic Ocean sea ice would eventually result in the extinction of the Polar Bear population which is dependent on the sea ice for their food supply hunting grounds.

In what may be the most outrageous prediction of "An Inconvenient Truth", Gore illustrates the complete melting of all of the Arctic sea ice as well as all of the Greenland glacial ice, resulting in an interruption of the deep ocean thermohaline circulation which would cause a mini Ice Age to occur in Europe.

Gore also jumped on the Katrina bandwagon (that is a full wagon!) by predicting that Katrina was an indication of things to come, from the increased hurricane intensity that will result from global warming.

In 2009 at a UN Conference on climate change, Al Gore predicted that with global warming having reached an "unbridled pitch", the north pole might be completely ice free in the summer of 2014.

Facts:

The 10-year "point of no return" that Mr. Gore predicted in 2006 came, and quietly went in January 2016. There has been no planetary crisis or environmental catastrophe. In fact, as has been documented, there has been no warming of the global average surface temperature since 1997, a period of 20 years.

The Arctic sea ice did not entirely melt, and the north pole was not ice free in summer 2014. Furthermore the north pole will not be "ice free" in the foreseeable future. The sea ice in the summer of 2014 actually expanded compared to the extent in 2012-2013 and was within the average range of the prior 50 years. The Arctic Sea ice seasonal pattern is to grow during the winter months of December through March, and the ice field partially melts between April and September when the sun is stronger in the northern hemisphere. The minimum ice level at the end of the summer is historically about 50% of the size of the maximum ice level in the winter season, so the normal seasonal growth and contraction (melt) pattern is substantial. The polar bear population is doing quite well. That fact is well known by the seals that the prey upon, as well as the beluga whales that frequently become trapped by ice field ponds in the rapidly refreezing Arctic sea ice.

Notwithstanding the numerous printed publications, film documentaries and public speeches produced and delivered by Al Gore on which he has made tens of millions of dollars in fees and royalty revenues, Mr. Gore has been entirely incorrect on all of his dramatic predictions of global warming environmental calamity. Given that he has literally gotten nothing right on this subject matter in 25 years, Al Gore has no credibility whatsoever, and he is in fact disingenuous. Al Gore is so misleading that I have dedicated an entire chapter in this book (chapter 8) to correcting all of his misleading propaganda on alleged global warming.

United Nations – IPCC

On May 4, 2007, during a meeting of climate scientists from UN member governments, The United Nations Intergovernmental Panel on Climate Change (UN IPCC) issued a statement that said, *"Governments are running out of time to address climate change and to avoid the worst effects of rising temperatures"*. The report went on to say that there are likely just "eight years left" to avoid the worst effects. *"Greater energy efficiency, renewable electricity sources and new technology to dump carbon dioxide underground, can all help to reduce greenhouse gas emissions"*, the scientists said. They went on to say that *"most of the technology needed to stop climate change in its tracks already exists, but that governments must act quickly to force through changes across all sectors of society"*. *"But there could be as little as eight years left to avoid a dangerous global average rise of 2C"* (two degrees Celsius = 3.6 degrees Fahrenheit).

Facts:

Well, the predicted eight years expired in May 2015, and there has been no change in the earth's average surface temperature, since 1997, a period of 20 years. Furthermore, the known change in the earth's average surface temperature has only been + 1.5 degrees Fahrenheit since 1850 (167 years).

So, the UN-IPCC's prediction was ridiculously wrong. The UN-IPCC had no prior historical rapid growth trend to point to, or any recent or current sudden temperature changes on which to base their very abrupt and absurd prediction. The UN scientists rely entirely on climate models that are based on very biased inputs and assumptions which drive the conclusion that the scientists intended. This is the tried and true playbook that is used by the man-made global warming theory advocates.

Their statement that "most of the technology needed to stop climate change in its tracks already exists", is beyond ridiculous. If this were true, the worldwide demand for fossil fuels that meet the energy needs of growing industrialization in developing nations, would not be at an all-time high. Solar and wind energy sources combined currently provide only 2.5% of the total energy demands.

The most shocking statement made by the UN scientists was, "*that governments must act quickly to force through changes across all sectors of society*". This statement, ladies and gentlemen should give you a chill.

This statement is at the core of why there is a global warming movement, and why the United Nations and the participating world governments, including the United States, is advocating the man-made global warming theory. If the government can control you and by control, I mean to heavily regulate and TAX the use of fossil fuels, they will have control over entire societies that would rival fascism, socialism or communism. I will come back to this very important issue in the next chapter.

(UN) - Entire Nations wiped off the earth by rising sea levels

On June 30, 1989, the San Jose Mercury News ran an article that quoted a senior environmental official at the United Nations, Noel Brown, saying "*entire nations could be wiped off the face of the earth by rising sea levels if global warming is not reversed by the year 2000". "Coastal flooding and crop failures would create an exodus of "eco-refugees," threatening political chaos"*, said Brown, director of the New York office of the U.N. Environment Program. He said governments have a 10-year window of opportunity to solve the greenhouse effect before it goes beyond human's ability to prevent this from happening.

Facts:

Obviously, Noel Brown director of the New York office of the U.N. Environment Program, wasn't even in the vicinity of reality with that delusional prediction. The year 2000 came and went 16 years ago, and the global sea levels continue to rise at a whopping 1.8 mm per year, or a pace of about one inch every 14 years.

But this is the common play book used by global warming activists. They make really loud, bold and scary predictions to scare the hell out of the average citizen who gets their news from the main stream media, which by the way backs all of these crazy theories as well.

Before we move on, let's agree on one thing – that the United Nations no longer has any credibility. The UN has demonstrated this spectacularly on numerous occasions. For example, in 2015 the UN appointed Saudi Arabia to chair the United Nations Human Rights Council. Saudi Arabia has one of the worst women's rights records in the world. Women in Saudi Arabia are not allowed to leave their home without a male guardian. They aren't allowed to drive a car. The state kills atheists, homosexuals and dissidents with public executions, and the UN made them the chair of the Human Rights Council. If it weren't so dangerous and preposterous, it would be comical.

The UN and its Intergovernmental Panel on Climate Change has been supporting hysterical climate catastrophe predictions since 1990, including melting of the Arctic sea ice, flooding of the eastern seaboard of the U.S., and the loss of global crop production and food supplies due to the alleged sudden rise in global surface temperatures.

One by one, their ridiculous predictions of catastrophe beyond any in world history in size and scope, have repeatedly come and gone. Nothing that they predict ever happens, and none of the climate characteristics that would have to happen to make their predictions a reality ever, even remotely materialize.

It is time to call the United Nations Intergovernmental Panel on Climate Change exactly what it is: a biased and dishonest single purpose organization that is trying to use the legitimate field of science to create a false narrative of exclusively human-caused global warming, whose goal is an international treaty that would mandate requirements on its member nations, that will result in taxation and other life altering modifications on the innocent citizens of the member nations, just for using fossil fuels in their everyday lives.

The UN wants to tax you, and tell you how to live your life. And if they get their way they will doom 1.6 billion human beings to a life of poverty with no hope of improved living conditions, while living in a world with the possibility to make their lives better. As Nancy Reagan once said, "just say No!".

Stephen Hawking – Physicist

This last example of liberal lunacy is really, just sad. In a July 2017 interview, Stephen Hawking made comments in reaction to the news that President Donald Trump had announced that the United States would withdraw from the Paris Climate Agreement. Mr. Hawking said that *"President Trump's decision could make the Earth become like Venus, with a temperature of over 250 degrees and raining sulfuric acid"*. Hawking also said that *"Trump will cause damage to our beautiful planet, and that we are close to the tipping point where global warming becomes irreversible"*.

Mr. Hawking continued, by saying that *"climate change is one of the great dangers we face"*, and he said, *"by denying the evidence for climate change, and pulling out of the Paris Climate Agreement, Donald Trump will cause avoidable environmental damage to our beautiful planet, endangering the natural world for us and our children"*.

Facts:

The atmosphere of Venus is very hot and thick. You would not survive a visit to the surface of the planet, as you couldn't breathe the air. You would be crushed by the enormous weight of the atmosphere, and you would burn up in surface temperatures high enough to melt lead. The atmosphere of Venus is one of the hottest places in the solar system. If you were on the surface of Venus, the air above you would be about 90 times heavier than the Earth's atmosphere. This is similar to what a submarine experiences at 3,000 feet below the surface of the Earth's ocean. Thick clouds of sulfuric acid literally cover Venus. The atmosphere of Venus is in no way comparable to the Earth's atmosphere.

The earth's surface has not experienced temperatures as hot as 250 degrees, as Mr. Hawking referenced, since billions of years ago during the early formation of the planet and the earth's atmosphere.

Mr. Hawking's comments are literally absurd. For someone of his intellect to make such a ridiculous assertion is either an indication that at 75 years old he is losing his mental faculties, or that global warming is such a religious belief for him, that he is willing to say anything to support the cause, even if it embarrasses him on a personal and intellectual level. In either case, Stephen Hawking has no credibility left on this issue.

So far, the global warming activists have a batting average of 0.000 in the predictions of global warming calamities. They literally haven't gotten a single prediction right yet. That is because there is no global warming climate crisis.

Chapter Five

Who Is Behind It, And What Do They Want?

You don't have to be a conspiracy theory nut wearing a homemade tin foil hat with an antenna on top of it to understand what I am about to explain to you. The hard part of accepting this explanation is that the average citizen who works 40 hours a week just trying to make a living, and take care of their family, and maybe save a little money for a vacation and for their retirement...does not have either the time or the inclination to read about this subject matter and to really understand what is going on in this part of the political activism world that they don't have regular contact with.

The President of the United States is limited to two, four year terms in office. The members of Congress do not have such term limits. The Congressmen elected to the House of Representatives serve a term of two years, after which they must be re-elected by their district, however there is no limit to how many times they can be re-elected. The members of the Senate are elected to serve a term of six years, after which they must re-run in their District. Like the House members, there is no limit to how many times they can be re-elected.

Ok, let me just get my tin foil hat on...ok, my antenna is pointing up, and the hat is on straight, I'm looking in the mirror...and now I am ready! So, hear it is: The job of the United States government is to separate you the tax payer from as much of your money as they possibly can. Do you doubt that? That is why they have the Internal Revenue Service! Now, once "the government" has separated you from your money, the job of the members of the U.S. House of Representatives, and the members of the U.S. Senate (distinguished as they may be) is to spend as much of the tax payer's money as they possibly can. You see, spending tax payer money is the ultimate way for the leaders elected to the Congress to build up their power and influence. To borrow a powerful phrase from a famous man, "don't doubt me".

I will give you an example that illustrates all of this. The Federal government uses a budgeting methodology called "The Current Services Baseline". Before I explain that, let me just say...that the term "Federal Budget" is an *oxymoron*. Ok, moving on. When you set your budget for your family, the budget has certain essential items that you always include out of necessity, such as the mortgage, the utility bills, food, transportation, and of course the cell phone plan. Right?? And if your income allows for more, then you add on discretionary spending like new clothes, entertainment spending, and planning for vacations. Every year you adjust your budget up or down as needed, based on your income. That is just a basic principal that we call "reality", if you want to preserve your credit rating and protect your assets.

The Federal Government doesn't work like that, at all. The current services baseline simply means, when a government agency starts planning the budget for the next fiscal year, they *start* with the amount that they spent in the prior year. And then they build on from there. And just think of the logic. If the government agency needed that much money last year, then the government agency is going to need at least that much money next year, right? So, what this means is that the government budget, of which every single agency, administration and department uses the current services baseline, by proxy that budget amount never goes down. It can only go higher.

Let me give you a "real world" example to help you understand how this actually works. Remember in 2008 when we had a really bad recession in the U.S. economy? A bunch of big businesses were basically failing and the government was worried that the recession would become a depression if we didn't stabilize the financial markets. Stating it simplistically the government bailed out some very big businesses through mergers, sales or restructures, including names like Fannie Mae, Freddie Mac, American International Group ("AIG"), Lehman Brothers, and of course we can't forget good old General Motors ("GM"). By the way, if you haven't seen "The Big Short", you should check that out.

Ok, moving on. In the first year of Barack Obama's Presidency, the economy was still reeling from the 2008 recession. Being a good progressive liberal, President Obama created a stimulus package ("The American Recovery and Reinvestment Act of 2009 (ARRA)") that was intended to provide an economic stimulus, to help the U.S. economy to recover (in theory) from the 2008 recession. The cost of the stimulus program was included in the 2009 Federal budget.

The primary objective of the Stimulus package was to save existing jobs and create new ones as soon as possible. Other objectives were to provide temporary relief programs for those most affected by the recession and to "invest" in infrastructure, education, health, and renewable energy. So, by definition this package was a one-time, extraordinary "investment" intended to boost the economy back to health. Kind of like a surgery for a sick patient. It wasn't intended to be a yearly program, because if the stimulus worked, then the economy would recover and become healthy again, just like the genius Obama administration economic advisors had intended. The original amount of the stimulus package was about $800 billion. That is almost a *Trillion dollars*! So again, in theory you wouldn't expect the $800 billion one-time investment to be made the next year, and every year after that. Right?

Here is a summary of the federal budget spending totals from 2007 through 2011:

2007 -- $2.8 Trillion

2008 -- $2.9 Trillion

2009 -- **$3.5 Trillion**

2010 -- $3.6 Trillion

2011 -- $3.8 Trillion

And right there in black & white is the simple and perfect illustration of just what in the heck is wrong with the Federal budget. The primary difference between the 2008 budget and the 2009 budget is the $800 billion stimulus package, which was supposed to be a one-time, extraordinary investment intended to boost the economy back to health.

But because of the Current Services Baseline budget methodology, every penny spent in the prior year is "baked in" to the next year's budget amount. Therefore the $800 billion stimulus package has effectively been added in to the annual Federal budget in every year since The American Recovery and Reinvestment Act of 2009 (ARRA). That is waste, fraud and abuse. And it is insane irresponsibility. If you ran your home budget this way, you would go bankrupt, unless you can print money.

The EPA (Environmental Protection Agency) makes a living off this budgeting tactic. And, since it is practically impossible to get rid of a rank and file employee of the federal government, the agency just keeps growing and growing. The EPA is the very powerful federal enforcement arm that does the bidding of the radical and intolerant environmental activists. If you oppose a costly, unfair and overly restrictive environmental regulation, you will be accused of wanting polluted air, dirty water and contaminated soil. You will be branded as an enemy of the environment, and of being in the pocket of big business, or of the most evil, big oil.

Now I have to pull my tin foil conspiracy hat down real good and tight because this is the really difficult part. If you are like me, you won't like this part, but it is important so please read on. Because I love the United States of America, and I am thankful that I was so blessed to be born an American, I find it hard to believe that there are a lot of Americans who don't like America. They don't like America as it was founded. These people are called "liberals". Not Democrats per se. That is a political party with many points of view and varied beliefs. When I say "liberals" I am talking about an ideology. Liberal progressives (like Barack Obama) do not like America. Some of them even hate America. Liberals want to, and they are trying to, change America fundamentally. A lot of these liberal progressive Americans who don't like America, work in the government and in the main stream press. I believe that it is the liberal "hatred of America" that essentially got Donald J. Trump elected President in 2016, because his campaign theme was to "Make America Great Again"!

The American colonies fought the revolutionary war to escape the tyranny and oppression by King George III and the British Empire. They fought against the greatest military of their time to gain the right to individual freedom and liberty. Once they won the revolutionary war, they built the country with rugged individualism, because there was no other way to survive.

Rugged individualism today means that you accept responsibility for your life, and that what happens to you depends largely on your hard work and achievement. It means that you have in this country, all the freedom and opportunity in the world to make the most of your life. It doesn't mean that life is always fair for everyone.

Liberals don't like this concept of rugged individualism and personal responsibility because it goes against the basis of their ideology which is fairness, equality, sharing, compassion, and non-discrimination, which is to be provided by an all-powerful central government. Liberals believe in the assimilation of groups based on race, gender, sexual orientation, and country of origin. Liberals are more aligned with the principals of the state under communism or socialism, than they are with the principles of our Constitution (Life, Liberty, and the Pursuit of Happiness).

Liberals value the group (which they control) over the individual.

There are several layers of political elite liberals that exist in the universities of America, in the media, in "think tanks", and worst of all in the federal government. These liberal elites are very serious about their ideology, and they are doing everything in their power to change the minds of Americans to think the way that they do. The leaders of the liberal ideology movement use "causes" to promote "unity" such as that of the needs of the oppressed working class (communism), and of the desire to achieve social progress and equality through government actions and policies (socialism).

The principles of socialism and communism were greatly tarnished a couple of decades ago when the Soviet Union collapsed under the weight of an unsustainable social and economic model. Then came the economic reforms in communist China. So, the liberals took up the cause of militant environmentalism, and the biggest trophy in that movement was global warming. With global warming, the liberals found a tool with which they can potentially harness the power of the federal government to substantially control the daily way of life of the masses in America.

I am not saying that the silly Hollywood elites who are constantly trumpeting the alarms about the alleged dangers and catastrophes to come because of global warming, are trying to take over America. They are just repeating the party line because it makes them feel good, because they think they are "doing the right thing" to "save the world". Who doesn't want to save the world? And there are millions of well-meaning and very naïve Americans who buy into the theory because they are star struck by the celebrities, and they don't have any real knowledge of the subject of global warming (or the lack thereof) other than what they see and hear on the evening news or through entertainment news.

What I am saying is that the liberal elites who are in positions of power in the media and in the government, DO have the ability to influence the opinions of the voting masses, and they have the access to the power of the federal government through legislation and through regulations of the EPA. In June 2007, the former President of The Czech Republic Vaclav Klaus wrote an article for "The Financial Times" in which he said, "*As someone who lived under communism for most of his life, I feel obliged to say that I see the biggest threat to freedom, democracy, the market economy and prosperity now in ambitious environmentalism, not in communism. This ideology wants to replace the free and spontaneous evolution of mankind by a sort of central (now global) planning*".

When your goal is power and control, there is no greater tool than the power to ration something that everyone needs every day. Other than the need for food, the most powerful and effective way to control Americans is the power to ration energy. Every person and every business needs energy for everything that they do every single day. The goal is to tell you what kind of light bulbs you can use, the temperature that you are allowed to set on your thermostat, and how much you can travel. If you think that sounds ridiculous, the radicals inside the global warming movement are already at work devising methods of such control. (put your tin foil hat on, if you doubt me!) For example, the British parliament has already studied and discussed a proposal, that every citizen be required to carry a carbon card that must be presented, under penalty of law, when buying gasoline, traveling by airplane or using electricity. The card would contain your yearly carbon ration to be drawn down with every purchase, every trip, every swipe. If you exceed your carbon allowance you will pay a penalty (a tax).

In the United States, the economic model for centralized government control over energy use that has been discussed and considered is called "cap and trade". Under the cap and trade model the federal government would determine the allowable level of greenhouse gas emissions, meaning carbon dioxide emissions from the use of gasoline, electricity and other fuels. Companies that produce less than the total greenhouse gases that they have been allowed to emit would be permitted to sell their excess allowance (the "trade" part of cap & trade) to companies that have exceeded their emissions allowance. Companies that produce more total greenhouse gases than they have been allowed would have to pay a penalty (a tax) for exceeding the allowance (the "cap" part of cap & trade), if they have not purchased additional greenhouse gas emission allowance credits.

You may be wondering how a cap and trade penalty on companies that essentially are "breaking the law" is a bad thing. How, after all does that affect you? The answer is that it will affect you directly! If factories, airlines, shipping companies, railways and electric utilities are forced to spend money to reduce greenhouse gas emissions, or to pay greenhouse gas emission penalties, do you think they are just going to absorb those extra costs? No! They will pass those costs on to you, the consumer of their products. So, the government won't be "sticking it to big business and big oil". Ultimately the government will be sticking it to you! Don't doubt me.

And that's not all. It gets worse. The federal government would have to create a new agency to regulate and police the greenhouse gas cap and trade policy, similar to the Internal Revenue Service which enforces the collection of income and employment taxes. This new agency would establish, regulate, and enforce the greenhouse gas allowances for all of the businesses in America. Like any other major government regulation that has a dampening effect on business, cap and trade would raise the cost of doing business for all businesses and industries, and ultimately would result in job losses for individual Americans, as well as higher costs for gasoline, natural gas and electricity for every American consumer. It is always the little people who can least afford job losses, income reductions, or cost of living increases who get hurt first by big government regulations. Always.

And what is it that this new proposed tax and regulatory agency is trying to limit the use of? Obviously, the literal answer is the use of fossil fuels. But metaphorically speaking, it is the very benefits of the use of fossil fuels that have enriched the lives of humanity throughout the world, that would be negatively impacted. The use of coal, oil and natural gas give us fuel for our automobiles which provides mobility for access to jobs, the transport of products to fuel domestic and international commerce, chemicals and medicines that improve our quality of life, and have extended the life expectancy of people. The ability to have clean running water, and plumbing that allows for the sanitary removal of human wastewater. The production and availability of plentiful and affordable food for the population.

All of these good and life sustaining things and processes would be impacted and the availability would be limited, and the costs would be increased. In plain English, the very citizens who are naively convinced that they are causing something "bad", that they are not causing, will be made to pay the cost of that which is not happening! And at the end of the day American's freedom, liberty and income will be weakened even further than they already are. Now you know about the liberals, and what their political and economic motivations are to control you and your money. Now you need to know about The United Nations (The "UN").

The United Nations is an organization made up of member nations of the world, and its purpose is to promote international cooperation and maintain international order. It was established in October 1945 after World War II, in order to prevent another such conflict. When it was founded there were 51 member nations. The UN membership has grown to 193 nations. The headquarters of the UN is in Manhattan, New York City. The UN is financed by assessments of its member nations. These assessments are voluntary contributions by the members. Its objectives include maintaining international peace and security, promoting human rights, fostering social and economic development, protecting the environment, and providing humanitarian aid in cases of famine, natural disaster, and armed conflict.

The UN has an organization called "The Intergovernmental Panel on Climate Change" (IPCC). The IPCC is a scientific and intergovernmental body under the banner of the United Nations set up at the request of member governments, dedicated to the task of providing the world with an "objective", "scientific" view of climate change and its political and economic impacts.

The IPCC produces reports that support the "United Nations Framework Convention on Climate Change" (UNFCCC), which is the main international treaty on climate change. The ultimate objective of the UNFCCC is to "*stabilize greenhouse gas concentrations in the atmosphere at a level that would prevent dangerous anthropogenic (i.e., human-induced) interference with the climate system*".

With that simple statement from the UN charter for the IPCC, the UN eliminated any illusion of objectivity of the

IPCC. Clearly the IPCC is approaching its scientific study and reporting with the baseline assumption that any variation in the global climate is due to "anthropogenic" (human-caused) emissions of CO_2. The IPCC has no interest in studying the potential for natural causes of any changes in the global climate.

In November of 2009 a scandal was revealed to the public when a collection of email messages, data files and data processing programs were leaked by whistleblowers in the Climatic Research Unit at The University of East Anglia in the United Kingdom. The scandal became known as "ClimateGate". The leaked information revealed scientific fraud and data manipulation by scientists concerning the global warming theory, and raised questions about the assumptions used in the climate models regarding anthropogenic (man-made) global warming. The legitimacy of climate science and the theory that claims that humans are causing global warming was severely besmirched by ClimateGate.

The ClimateGate information leaked from the Climatic Research Unit at The University of East Anglia revealed how all the data centers worldwide, including NOAA and NASA in the United States, had conspired in the manipulation of global temperature records to suggest that temperatures in the 20th century rose faster and higher than they actually did. The selectivity of certain data and the exclusion of other undesired results made NASA's data and climate change conclusions biased to advance the anthropogenic (human caused) global warming agenda. ClimateGate revealed that climate scientists conspired to cover up research results that challenged the anthropogenic (human caused) global warming theory. The ClimateGate scandal was not reported by the American main stream media.

The Kyoto Protocol

In December 1997, representatives for more than 150 nations met in Kyoto, Japan, to negotiate the terms of the "Kyoto Protocol", a global climate agreement under the United Nations "Framework Convention on Climate Change". The "Framework Convention on Climate Change" is an international environmental treaty produced at the United Nations Conference on Environment and Development (UNCED), informally known as the "Earth

Summit", which was held in Rio de Janeiro in June of 1992. In layman's terms, it was step one by the UN to find a way to tax American citizens for their use of fossil fuels in their everyday lives.

The Kyoto Protocol was a comprehensive plan to reduce six greenhouse gas emissions, including carbon dioxide (CO_2), between 2008 and 2012. During the negotiations, President Bill Clinton pledged that, in those five years, the United States would reduce emissions by seven percent below 1990 levels. However, developing countries would not be held to the same standards as industrialized countries like the United States. In addition, there was no certainty that meeting the targets for reducing greenhouse gas emissions, would have any impact on CO_2 concentrations or on alleged global warming. Various economic analyses estimated that the treaty's restrictions would seriously damage the U.S. economy.

Concerns about the impact of the treaty were so great that on July 25, 1997, the U.S. Senate voted (95-0) to pass Senate Resolution 98 (S. Res. 98), known as the "Byrd-Hagel resolution", which stated that the Senate would not ratify the treaty unless (1) all nations under the treaty would be subject to the same requirements as were required of the United States, and (2) evidence must be provided showing that the treaty would not result in serious harm to the U.S. economy.

President Bill Clinton agreed to the Kyoto Protocol, and had Vice President Al Gore to sign the agreement on behalf of the United States in November 1998. However, the treaty required ratification by the Senate to become binding. Even though the Clinton administration signed the treaty, it was never submitted to the Senate for ratification, because it would have been "dead on arrival". When George W. Bush was elected the U.S. President in 2000, he opposed the Kyoto treaty, because "it exempted developing countries, including major population centers such as China and India, from compliance, and because it would cause serious harm to the U.S. economy". The Kyoto Protocol never became a binding agreement on any UN member nation.

The Paris Agreement

The Paris Agreement is the successor agreement to the Kyoto Protocol. The language of the Paris agreement was negotiated by representatives of 195 countries at the 21st Conference of the Parties of the Framework Convention on Climate Change (UNFCCC) in Paris and adopted by "consensus" of the UN members on December 12, 2015.

Unlike the failed Kyoto Protocol, which aimed to set commitment targets that would have "legal force", the Paris Agreement relies solely on "consensus-building", and it allows each member voluntary and nationally self-determined targets. The specific climate goals are politically encouraged, rather than legally bound. Only the processes governing the reporting and review of goals are mandated under international law. This structure is especially notable for the United States, because there are no legal "mitigation or finance" targets. The agreement is considered an "executive agreement" rather than a treaty. In other words, this treaty is *not binding on anyone.*

The UN expressed its displeasure with the nature of the non-binding agreement with this statement: *"the stated objectives of the Paris Agreement are implicitly predicated upon an assumption – that member states of the United Nations, including high polluters such as China, the U.S.,*

India, Brazil, Canada, Russia, Indonesia and Australia, which generate more than half the world's greenhouse gas emissions, will somehow drive down their carbon pollution voluntarily and assiduously without any binding enforcement mechanism to measure and control CO_2 emissions at any level from factory to state, and without any specific penalty gradation or fiscal pressure (for example a carbon tax) to discourage bad behavior".

From "factory to state"? That is a scary and ominous reference. Pay attention to the meaning of these words people, please! And how about the reference to "high polluters"? I remind you that carbon dioxide (CO2), which is the "pollution" to which the UN is referring, is a colorless, odorless gas produced by burning carbon and organic compounds and by human and animal respiration. It is naturally present in the air and is absorbed by plants in photosynthesis. Carbon Dioxide is not a poison or a pollutant. It is essential for the well-being of all life on earth!

There is an inherent tendency in every organization toward self-preservation. In the case of the UN that tendency is for the UN to gain the ultimate power over its most powerful member: to have a legally binding treaty that allows the UN to regulate environmental activities in the United States, with the power to tax directly the citizens and businesses of the world's most dynamic economy.

During a May 4, 2007, meeting of climate scientists from UN member governments, The United Nations Intergovernmental Panel on Climate Change (UN IPCC) stated that "*Governments are running out of time to address climate change and to avoid the worst effects of rising temperatures*". They went on to say that "*governments must act quickly to force through changes across all sectors of society*". I cannot emphasize any stronger for you the reader, just what the ultimate goal of the United Nations is. What do you think the UN means by "**force through changes across all sectors of society**"? That means that the UN wants the U.S. government to force the power to tax the U.S. economy for the use of fossil fuels, against the will of the American tax payers, by any means necessary. Again, to borrow a phrase from a very famous man, "don't doubt me".

Remember what I told you about "liberals". They are in this scandalous attempt to exert control over the American citizens use of fossil fuels, right along with and in full support of the UN's efforts. New York Times columnist Thomas Friedman, the author of the book "Hot, Flat and Crowded: Why we need a green revolution", wrote a column in which he discussed his fervent desire for, *"our government to get its act together and launch a green revolution with the same persistent focus and direction that China does through authoritarian means"*. Authoritarian means? If you need that translated, it means he wants the government to act against the will of the people. This is the talk of fascism!

These liberals are embedded in the university campuses of America where they are literally brain washing our college students. And they are everywhere in the main stream media. Here is another very obvious example, of a media embed that is spouting the global warming theory. Have you heard of Bill Nye? Bill Nye "the Science Guy". This guy is a real piece of work. He hosted a television show on PBS in the late nineties called *"Bill Nye the Science Guy".* It was an educational television program which aimed to teach science to a preteen audience. Bill Nye is not actually a scientist, but was educated as a mechanical engineer.

In April 2017 Bill Nye appeared as a guest on a segment on CNN to discuss "Earth Day". Also appearing in the segment was William Happer, a Princeton professor of physics. Mr. Happer opposes the view of anthropogenic global warming, and he believes that more carbon dioxide in the atmosphere and modest climate warming will actually bring benefits from increased agricultural yields worldwide, and the greening of the planet, that far outweigh any harm. And, for the record I agree with Professor Happer.

During the panel debate of the issue of global warming, Mr. Happer stated that carbon dioxide is not a pollutant. *"There's this myth that's developed around carbon dioxide that it's a pollutant,"* Happer said. *"But you and I both exhale carbon dioxide with every breath. Each of us emits about two pounds of carbon dioxide a day, so are we polluting the planet?"* Nye replied *"what he claims to not understand is the rate. It's the speed at which we're adding carbon dioxide."* *"What you got to get is the speed at which things are changing."* Happer replied saying that

"Earth's temperature is not rising nearly as fast as the alarmists' computer models predicted." Professor Happer then added: *"The whole basis for the alarmism is not true. It's based on flawed computer modeling."* Nye replied, *"That's completely wrong. Say what you will, but you have it absolutely wrong."* Nye also said to Mr. Happer, *"Sir, with some respect, I encourage you to cut this out so that we can all move forward and make the United States a world leader in technology."*

Having been entirely ineffective in the debate with Mr. Happer, and in complete frustration, Nye then said to the CNN host *"I will say, as much as I love the CNN, you're doing a disservice by having one climate change skeptic, and not 97 or 98 scientists or engineers concerned about climate change,"* referring to the so-called "consensus" among scientists that climate change is real, and primarily caused by human activity. So, if Bill Nye has his way CNN should conduct their global warming discussions in the environment of fascism, where differing opinions are not allowed, like in Nazi Germany and Italy during World War II.

Are you still wearing your tin foil conspiracy hat? I know that for the average person who "has a life", and doesn't focus on these mundane political issues, this chapter has been some heavy reading. It's not fun to be told that a bunch of your fellow Americans, including some of your elected leaders and prominent media members, basically hate America. And, your friendly neighborhood UN wants to usurp power and money from your country.

The ultimate goal of the leaders of the global warming movement both inside our government and at the UN, is to get more of the American taxpayer's money. That means you. This is personal. A UN tax on the United States of America would be a way to take money from a producer nation and give it to the socialists and the communists to help prop of their failing economic systems. Redistribution of wealth is a central tenant of liberalism. The high standard of living that we enjoy as American's is unparalleled in the world and is unprecedented in the history of mankind. Many of the well-meaning global warming sympathizers have been fooled by these crafty liberals into thinking that they're actually helping to avert a global catastrophe, by changing your way of life.

Don't fall for it. There is no climate crisis, and there is nothing wrong with living your life in America.

The liberals who say America is bad because we use more resources than any other nation, are the same ones who board a big jet and fly home after they make their political speech bashing America. They ignore the fact that the United States of America is the biggest producing economy on the planet. We feed the world and we pollute much less than the communist, socialist, and totalitarian nations that the UN wants to tax us for.

Don't get sucked in by the propaganda. Global warming is not a crisis, and it is not your fault. Once you understand the political game that is being played, and the goal to take more of your money, it should all start to make more sense to you.

I am going to give you 10 irrefutable facts that prove that the so-called man-made global warming crisis is a hoax:

Fact 1 - The global average surface temperature has risen only 1.5 degrees Fahrenheit in the last 167 years; about 2/3 of that increase happened between 1850 and 1940, before the industrial CO2 emissions grew materially, and there has been absolutely no warming in the last 20 years while CO2 emissions have been the highest in human history.

Fact 2 - There has been no systematic increase in the frequency or the intensity of hurricanes in the US during the last century; hurricane activity has been below the historical average since 2005.

Fact 3 - Despite the fact that there are relatively frequent droughts in certain parts of the US (California & Texas) throughout recorded history there is no empirical evidence of an increase in the frequency or the length of droughts. Drought prone areas are experiencing droughts at the same historical rate.

Fact 4 - After a brief receding of about 10 percent of the Arctic sea ice from 2005 to 2012, the sea ice extent has recovered to the 1979 satellite image extent. Sea ice seasonal melt and refreeze are at historic seasonal norms. There will be NO commercial shipping in the Northwest Passage, even in the summer season.

Fact 5 - The Greenland glacial ice is not melting beyond the seasonal and decadal variance norms. The Antarctic Ice cap (south pole) is growing!

Fact 6 – There is no empirical evidence of global sea level rise beyond the historical average of about 2mm per year.

Fact 7 - The combination of the cooling effect of evaporation, and the climate cooling effects of the global weather systems are cumulatively stronger than the greenhouse warming effect.

Fact 8 - In 1997 the United States Senate voted 95-0 to reject the Kyoto treaty. This is clear evidence that responsible leadership rejected the notion of any alleged climate crisis, and rejected the risk of significant harm to the U.S. economy.

Fact 9 - The Paris Agreement is non-binding against the UN member nations. No UN member nation has ever agreed to binding regulations regarding CO_2 emissions. This is clear evidence that the member nations are unwilling to sacrifice their living standards, for a non-existent climate crisis.

Fact 10 - The United Nations Intergovernmental Panel on Climate Change (UN IPCC) stated in May 2007 that "*governments must act quickly to force through changes across all sectors of society*". They know that there is no climate crisis, and that only through authoritarian force can they hope to tax Americans.

"Don't doubt me".

On June 1, 2017 President Donald J. Trump announced that the United States will withdraw from the Paris Climate Accord. Thank you, President Trump for your courage, common sense, and leadership.

Chapter Six

God's Solution - Earth's HVAC System

The United Nations Intergovernmental Panel on Climate Change was formed in 1988, and in June of 1989 the UNIPCC began its campaign of predicting global climate disasters because of alleged anthropogenic (man-made) global warming. The threats to mankind have repeatedly included predictions of more droughts, more floods, bigger and more frequent hurricanes, catastrophic rise in sea levels, drowning US coastal cities, and heightened global temperatures causing the devastation of world crops and food supplies, leading to famine and global geopolitical crisis. Oh, and the extinction of the polar bears.

Al Gore made numerous efforts to persuade the US Congress about the alleged ravages of global warming during the 1980s and 1990s. While serving as the Vice President, Al Gore strongly advocated for the ratification of the Kyoto Protocol in 1997, but the US Senate soundly rejected the UN sponsored treaty by a vote of 95-0. Then in 2006 Mr. Gore produced his documentary "An Inconvenient Truth" in which he has predicted every imaginable global disaster, from repeated category five super hurricanes, and unending droughts, to the melting of the polar ice caps causing inundation of the worlds coastal cities, all of which he characterized as "a nature hike through the book of revelations".

After listening to all these hyper hysterical predictions of doom, and never seeing anything of the sort materialize, I began to think that there must be more to the story than a bunch of activists who were just "getting it wrong". So, it became time to study all the issues including the weather patterns, the larger global climate and the politics of all of the people and organizations who were making themselves known. What I found out is that there indeed is a lot more going on here than meets the eye.

If you form your opinion about global warming from watching "An Inconvenient Truth", you will get a very simplistic explanation of how and why global warming is allegedly going to happen. And even if you don't take the time to watch "An Inconvenient Truth" you will still get this same opinion by listening to the main stream media, your college professors, high profile actors and entertainers, and of course former President Obama.

The global warming party line is that the sun's rays come through the earth's atmosphere and hit the earth's surface. Some of the sun's energy is absorbed by the ground and the oceans, and a portion of the sun's energy gets reflected back into the atmosphere, where the earth's greenhouse gases help to hold some of the energy in the atmosphere to keep the earth warm and livable. The global warming bad news theory is that the greenhouse gases have gotten much "thicker", because humans are driving cars and SUVs, and flying on jets, and generating electricity with coal or gas fired power plants, which is causing the emissions of carbon dioxide (CO2), or as Al Gore puts it "global warming pollution that's being put up there", which thickens the greenhouse gas blanket. The thicker greenhouse gas blanket allegedly causes more of the sun's energy to be reflected back to the earth's surface which theoretically causes global warming. This is the very simplistic global warming model. If that is all you know, then it can seem somewhat convincing and pretty scary.

But I have some good news for you. There really is "a lot more going on here than meets the eye". There is an entire system of very powerful forces that are working non-stop, 24 hours a day, every single day of every single year. This system will never stop working no matter what mankind does down here on the earth. Think of this system as "earth's HVAC system". We never have to repair it and it never breaks down. This "system" is called, <u>the weather</u>.

Weather includes all of the things that can happen every day on our earth including thunderstorms, windstorms, hail, lightning, floods, tornados, hurricanes, snowstorms, droughts, cloudy misty dreary days, and clear beautiful blue sky days. "Weather" is the stuff that happens every day where you live, and all around the world. "Climate" is the accumulation of all the weather stuff that happens over a long period of time. Weather can change from day to day, and weather can even change during a single day. Climate tends to follow largely repetitive patterns over time. For example, the seasons: fall, winter, spring, and summer.

The fundamental job of the earth's climate is to _get rid of excess heat_. The weather serves as the tool kit that allows the climate to move the heat around the earth, and to get rid of some of the heat when there is too much. This is why we have not seen any large increases in the earth's global average temperature, despite the increase in the carbon dioxide (CO_2) concentration in the atmosphere since the end of World War II. You probably haven't heard this explanation from Al Gore, or Leo DiCaprio, or the UN IPCC, or any of the other pop culture icons who repeat the global warming party line. But it is true that earth's HVAC system is working for us, all day, every day.

You might be wondering…well, if this "earth HVAC system" is working, then why do we have bad things happen in our weather? Such as potentially destructive weather including thunderstorms, windstorms, hail, lightning, floods, tornados, hurricanes, snowstorms, and droughts. Sometimes these weather events can make bad things happen to people and property. Well, the weather is part of a very large system. While the weather might seem "all relative" to you in the city or town where you are living, the weather is part of a global system that takes care of the entire planet. While the weather does a good job for the earth taken as a whole there can be some rough days on a local basis, "here and there". However, in the long run the system works out well "in the big picture" (controlling the climate).

Rather than just tell you that the weather is the earth's HVAC system, and that you don't need to worry about global warming, I am going to explain to you, very basically, how the weather system works.

The first step in the process of making weather is the sun. The sun emits a huge amount of energy. This energy travels through space in the form of short-wave radiation. Only a tiny portion of the Sun's power actually reaches the surface of the earth. The earth's land and oceans absorb the solar radiation (energy) and in turn emits terrestrial radiation (heat). So, the earth's atmosphere actually gets heated from the ground up. That is why a mountain climber will find colder temperatures as he/she climbs higher, even though he/she is moving closer to the sun.

When the Sun's energy is absorbed by the surface of the earth it causes the surface to warm up. The surface then emits some of the solar radiation back up into the atmosphere. If nothing else happened the surface of the earth would be so hot (about 140 degrees Fahrenheit), that it would be uninhabitable for humans. This is where the weather enters the equation.

The "troposphere" is the region of the earth's atmosphere where humans live. The troposphere goes from the earth's surface to about seven miles high. The air in the troposphere (all around you) is constantly moving in vertical and horizontal cycles (wind). The heat of the sun being absorbed and emitted by the earth's surface causes changes in the air pressure and the air temperature. These changes in the air pressure and temperature causes vertical air currents. If you have ever experienced a bumpy ride while flying on a jet, that is a vertical air current. When air heats up, the air becomes less dense and it rises up through the troposphere toward thinner air. As the warm air rises higher in the troposphere it reaches colder air, because the earth's upper atmosphere elevations are very cold. The air eventually cools back to a denser state and then it sinks back down towards the earth's surface. This is one simple example of weather cooling the earth's warm surface by removing excess heat.

There are different surface temperatures across the globe, and across our continental United States, and even across single states that have differing elevations. The sun does not provide the same heat to every part of the planet, and it does not shine on the whole earth at once. When it is daytime on one side of the world, it is night on the other side. While one city receives sun that is filtered down vertically through one atmosphere worth of air space, in other locations on the globe the sun has to travel at a more horizontal trajectory because the earth is round, and because the earth is rotating around the sun, and spinning on its axis continuously.

For example, Iceland sitting on the globe at 65 degrees North latitude and near the Arctic circle, will receive far less direct sunlight than Arizona, sitting at 34 degrees North latitude, and much closer to the equator. So, in some cities, the solar radiation is forced to filter through the equivalent of several atmospheres, because of the difference in the angle toward the sun. This is also why the sun appears far less bright at sunset than at high noon.

Temperature also varies from place to place due to the unequal cooling and heating of land and water. On a hot summer day when you walk in your bare feet to your backyard swimming pool, you will notice the hard surface around the pool is much hotter than the water in the pool. That is because it takes much longer for water to absorb heat than the ground. The ground absorbs heat quickly. The ground also reflects more heat back into the air above it. Now think of this example on the scale of the earth's oceans and continents. Altitude, geographic location, cloud cover and ocean currents all affect temperatures around the world.

When the air in one area heats up faster than the air in an adjacent area, the pressure differential generates <u>wind</u>.

Because of the rotation of the earth on its axis, wind in the northern hemisphere where the United States is located generally blows toward the east. Wind helps to move weather systems (and helps move excess heat) around the globe. But wind is only one of the tools of the weather tool box.

Air pressure is much higher at the poles, and is much lower at the equator. This causes a natural cycle of wind to flow from the poles toward the equator. In addition to the significant difference of air pressure at the poles, the planet is covered with many smaller areas of high and low pressure. These natural weather gradients generate additional wind on a regional scale as they move around, because high-pressure air always wants to flow into low-pressure areas, while at the same time being affected by the easterly wind direction of the northern hemisphere rotation. Wherever surface level winds meet the earth's surface, there is the potential for friction, which can slow and even redirect the flow of air. There are also localized conditions to consider wherever high and low, pressure weather systems meet. These can include coastlines, mountains, and valleys.

Water plays a major role in the weather, and in the important role of helping to control excess heat in the troposphere, even though water is such a small fraction of the atmosphere. Water can exist as a solid (ice), a liquid or a gas under normal atmospheric conditions, and it is the key player in the hydrologic cycle. In this cycle, water evaporates from the ocean in the form of water vapor and eventually returns to land and sea in the form of precipitation.

You can't see water vapor, but it becomes visible when it cools and condenses against a warm car window on a cool day. When water vapor condenses, it clings to tiny dust particles in the atmosphere. If there is enough cooling water vapor in the air, these tiny particles accumulate by the trillions to form clouds. The formation of clouds occurs when humid or water vapor filled air rises to an altitude in the troposphere where cooler temperatures force condensation.

If there was no wind, the water droplets would just fall right back down to the surface. But there is wind! So, the Earth's complex upper air winds keep the clouds afloat, moving them across long distances and altering their shape in the process. If enough water condenses around a particle, or if the air temperature drops the water will fall back to the surface. Liquid particles fall in the form of rain. Frozen particles fall as snow.

The ultimate job of the weather is to move excess heat from where it is to where it is needed. The wind, the clouds and the rain are all part of a very complex process that is continuously transferring excess heat. On a regional scale, the heat gets moved from sitting near the earth's surface to higher up in the atmosphere. On a global scale, the heat gets moved from the lower latitudes (the equator) to the higher latitudes (the polar regions).

Remember earlier we discussed that when there is a difference in temperature between one region and an adjacent region, this causes wind to blow across the surface of the earth. The wind picks up heat and takes it somewhere else (higher altitude, or higher latitude). The wind moves the excess heat in one of two ways. The first is "sensible heat" (a rise in the surface temperature). Sensible heat is the transfer of heat from the surface of the earth to the overlying air higher in the atmosphere. Sensible heat is related to changes in the temperature of a gas or object with no change in phase (liquid, gas or solid). The second is "latent heat". Latent heat is related to the changes in phase between liquids, gases, and solids.

With latent heat transfer, water is evaporated from the surface, which adds water vapor to the air. This is one of the most important phases of the weather system. Latent heat loss by the earth's surface through evaporation is the most dominant method of removing excess heat from the surface of the planet. "Latent" refers to the fact that the heat energy is not added to the air, but instead the energy is exhausted by the process of changing the water from its liquid form to a vapor form. *When the surface water is evaporated to form vapor, it removes heat from the surface*. The process of evaporation requires energy. The energy is exhausted. An example of this is when you are sitting by a lake or a pool, and your skin is wet. A breeze blowing on your skin feels cool. The water is stealing heat from your body so that it can turn into water vapor.

About 90 percent of the heat that is lost by oceans and lakes is through the energy that is required to evaporate water from the surface. Remember, that 71 percent of the earth's surface is covered by water. This explains how Latent heat loss by the earth's surface through evaporation is the most dominant method of removing excess heat. Evaporation occurs on land as well. The land evaporation occurs when water is cycled through plants and trees as part of the growing process, known as evapotranspiration.

To further illustrate the power of water in the climate, if there is no surface water or vegetation in a region, then all the sun's energy that is absorbed will be turned into sensible heat (a rise in the surface temperature). Without water to absorb some of the heat through evaporation all the energy goes into raising the temperature. An example of this is the "urban heat island effect" in large cities. Another example is the desert.

So, simplistically stated weather is a big repetitive cycle that moves excess heat "upward" (altitude in the troposphere) and "poleward" (to higher latitudes) to help cool the earth's surface. We have followed the movement of some of the heat from the earth's surface, to the wind blowing across the surface and picking up some of the heat, to the cloudy ascending air currents when heat is released by condensation, which causes rain (or snow), to the descending air currents of cold air from the upper troposphere.

This is the pathway by which heat is transferred from the earth's surface to the upper troposphere, cooling the surface. There is one more heat transfer process that helps to cool the surface of the planet.

Some of the heat that is absorbed by the earth's surface and then emitted back up into the troposphere does not get involved in the weather system. About 30 percent of the sun's radiation (energy) is reflected directly back out into outer space in the form of infrared radiation. The remaining 70 percent of the sun's radiation is used by the earth's atmosphere and the weather system to keep the earth habitably warm.

The weather systems cool the surface of the earth to a temperature that is well below what sunlight and the greenhouse effect are trying to make it. The cooling effects of the global weather systems are more powerful than, and have the ultimate controlling influence over, CO_2 and the total greenhouse warming effect. You have probably never heard this before, and you will never hear this from the global warming alarmists. But just use a little common sense...if this were not true, then wouldn't at least one or two of the failed predictions of global warming catastrophe that have been claimed for the last 30 years by the global warming alarmists, have happened? But they have not! Not one.

It is not by chance that the earth has a highly complex system of weather that is clearly adaptable to the circumstances of the ever-changing climate conditions. It is as if the earth's HVAC system has an automatic thermostat. The earth's HVAC system was not made by Carrier, Trane, Rheem, Lennox or York. The earth's HVAC system was designed, built, installed, and is being maintained by God. How else can you explain this literal miracle?

Genesis 1:1

In the beginning God created the heavens and the earth.

Genesis 1:3

And God said, "Let there be light", and there was light.

Genesis 1:9-11

And God said, "Let the water under the sky be gathered to one place, and let the dry ground appear". And it was so. God called the dry ground "land", and the gathered waters he called "seas". And God saw that it was good. Then God said, "let the land produce vegetation: seed-bearing plants and trees on the land that bear fruit with seed in it, according to their various kinds". And it was so.

There has not been any significant warming of the climate, as has been hysterically predicted for the last 50 years. As I have stated before, and this is not in dispute, the global average surface temperature has increased by just 1.5 degrees in the last 167 years. But that alone is not the story. The real story is that about two-thirds (66.6%) of the global average surface temperature increase took place before 1940, when only 12.5% of the incremental human CO_2 emissions were occurring. That is a pretty good indication that natural factors are causing the temperature change, not man-made CO2 emissions.

So, you may be thinking, well there will be a big increase in temperature later (after 1940) when the CO2 emissions start increasing a lot. The facts just don't support that because between 1940 and 1970 the global average surface temperature actually *declined* by <0.36> degrees Fahrenheit. During those 30 years the global CO2 emissions increased, and 19% of all human CO2 emissions since the industrial revolution began were produced, yet the temperature declined. During the decade of the 1970s there were numerous articles published in Time Magazine and many other famous publications that warned of a coming "Ice Age". Many of these same publications have since jumped on the global warming scare wagon.

There has been no global warming at all during the last 20 years, during which 27% of the CO2 emissions in the history of mankind have been emitted! So clearly, there is something in the global climate system other than CO2 emissions that is influencing the climate, and the global average surface temperature. Something that is more powerful, and adaptable, and divinely inspired.

Isaiah 40:21

Do you not know? Have you not heard?

Has it not been told you from the beginning?

Have you not understood since the earth was founded?

What I have called in simple layman's terms the "earth's HVAC system" is in fact a very powerful atmospheric circulation system. Wind picks up the excess heat from the earth's surface, and releases the heat as it rises through the troposphere in huge precipitation systems, and then flows away from the precipitation systems and sinks and cools before it reaches the earth's surface, where it starts the entire circulation process all over again.

While this illustration of the circulation system might seem limited to a small region in reality these circulations extend for thousands of miles. On a very large scale, warm moist air is picked up from the tropics, and this warm air rises not straight up but at an angle, and travels thousands of miles to reach the upper troposphere. These tropical air flows are called "extratropical cyclones", and their main purpose is to carry excess heat from the tropics (the area around the equator) to the higher latitudes. Why do you think that none of the often-predicted climate catastrophes have ever happened? Hmmm?

These circulation systems that cycle hot air from the tropics to the poles and then take cooler air back to the tropics, are running on a global basis non-stop. The atmosphere is continuously overturning and flowing and constantly removing excess heat from the surface and moving it high in the atmosphere, and also carrying it from tropical latitudes where the most sunlight is absorbed, to the poles where the least sunlight is absorbed. All of these continuous air circulations in the atmosphere combined with the very complex and cyclical weather systems, work together to accomplish one wonderful and miraculous purpose: to move excess heat from where there is more, to where there is less.

The variable of the earth's HVAC system that automatically "adjusts the thermostat" is the combination of clouds and precipitation. Contrary to the opinion of Al Gore and the UN climate scientists, the strength of the greenhouse effect is not an independent and static quantity, even though it is measured as a quantity ("PPM"). The greenhouse effect is under the control of the weather processes. Warming will be relatively mild and stable because the climate system balances itself in reaction to the warming impact of the increasing greenhouse gases (the CO2). Weather systems determine how much of the sunlight the climate system will use before the clouds will basically turn off the solar energy supply before it ever reaches the greenhouse gas blanket.

Genesis 1: 27-28

*So God created man in his own image, in the image of God he created him; male and female he created them. God blessed them and said to them, "be fruitful and increase in number, **fill the earth and subdue it**. Rule over the fish of the sea and the birds of the air and over every living creature that moves on the ground".*

The facts that we have discussed so far have dispelled the myths that the climate is in distress, and that the climate is fragile and in danger of being harmed by human activities. Now we need to set the record straight about the benefits of the modern oil and gas resources that fuel our lives and economies. The oil and gas resources that the modern oil industry pulls from the depths of the earth are a gift from God. God has provided everything that mankind needs to live on this fabulous planet, and if managed right, to live well. While mankind survived for a very long time before the discovery of oil, the quality of life has improved by a quantum leap since the full measure of the modern oil and gas industry has developed.

Isaiah 45:18

For this is what the Lord says, he who created the heavens, he is God; He who fashioned and made the earth, he founded it;

He did not create it to be empty, but formed it to be inhabited;

He says, I am the Lord, and there is no other.

Human life has existed on this planet for about 6 million years. The early human existence was extremely primitive and very harsh. During the stone age (2.5 million years ago) humans lived in caves and jungles, and their daily existence revolved around gathering food, and trying to avoid being killed and eaten by larger animals. The life expectancy if you survived birth, was about 18 years.

During the bronze age humans had tools to make things that improved the quality of life somewhat over the stone age. There were wood framed structures to live in that provided shelter from the elements. They learned to use horses and carts to improve mobility and farming production. The life expectancy improved to about 30 years, on average.

During the iron-age more tools and weapons were developed. Farming improved further with ploughs that were pulled by oxen. But life was still very difficult. Most people spent their days laboring in the farm fields to produce enough food to survive the winter. Firewood was used for warmth and cooking. Farming was extremely laborious, difficult, and inefficient. Families provided basically for themselves.

Around 1750 the early industrial revolution began in Europe. This resulted in millions of people moving from farms in the open countryside, to large cities, seeking the new industrial jobs and a better way of life. For example, the population of

London grew from about 1 million in 1800 to over 6.5 million in 1900.

The early industrial revolution was fueled by coal fired steam engines. The productivity of the early factories was 50X to 100X higher than the prior productivity of non-mechanized human labor. This was great for the factory owners, and they got very wealthy. The existence for the common workers was very harsh, as they worked 12 to 16 hour days, and at low wages. The working conditions were grueling, dangerous, and dirty. However, life expectancy during this early industrial era improved to an average of 45 years, a 50% increase over the iron age.

The use of coal begat the steel industry. As a material, steel combines high tensile strength with low cost. Steel is one of the building blocks of American industry. Steel making is an energy-intensive business, in which technology advances have reduced the energy requirement by 60% over the last 50 years.

Coal is a primary feedstock for steel. You cannot make steel in a blast furnace without coal. Approximately 70% of global steel output is produced in blast furnaces which require metallurgical coal. Coking Coal, or Metallurgical coal is used in manufacturing steel, where carbon must be as stable and ash-free as possible. Coking coal is also heated to produce coke, a hard-porous material which is used to blast in furnaces for the extraction of iron from the iron ore.

For the greenies out there, you cannot make wind turbines without coal. It takes about 220 tons of coal (both metallurgical and thermal coal) to produce a wind turbine.

The United States has more coal than any other nation on the planet, with about 28% of the entire world's recoverable reserves. Now that we know the whole truth about the hoax of global warming from CO2 emissions, because of the balancing effects of the earth's weather systems (aka: the earth's HVAC system) over the greenhouse effect, America's coal reserves are a mighty asset, and an energy supply.

Twenty five percent of the United States electric power plants are coal fired. The United States also needs to return to a position of leadership in the production of steel, with American coal.

Isaiah 40:12

Who has measured the waters in the hollow of his hand,

Or with the breadth of his hand marked off the heavens?

Who has held the dust of the earth in a basket,

Or weighed the mountains on the scales and the hills in a balance?

Oil was discovered in Pennsylvania in 1859. The internal combustion engine was invented shortly after that. Henry Ford started building the Model T in 1908. Gas powered farm machinery and implements were made available around 1920. Electricity became available to towns and cities in America during the 1930s. Refrigerators and televisions became common in U.S. households during the 1950s. Why was there all this innovation during the early and mid 20th century? Simple! Because of oil and all of its benefits and by-products!

Our modern economy, and the wonderful quality of life that we now enjoy is dependent on the energy provided by oil and gas. Every aspect of our lives are completely intertwined with the use of oil and gas and their by-products.

Oil and gas gives us efficient and affordable heat in the winter and air conditioning in the summer. Oil and gas gives us affordable electricity to light our homes and offices, to power our subways and elevators and computer networks. Can you imagine our wonderful healing and life-saving hospitals without affordable and plentiful oil, gas, and electricity?

We have affordable and plentiful gasoline for our cars, and yes our SUV's. That's right, I said it!!

We can fly on jets across the country in four hours, or across the globe in the same day! Great ocean going ships take products from one end of the world to the other providing life enhancing products where ports are available. Mile long trains are powered by mighty locomotives to transport goods and supplies from coast to coast, and everywhere in between. These treasures of the earth, oil and gas, are a blessing not a threat to survival.

The oil and gas industry is unfairly attacked and maligned because of the occasional accident that causes relatively temporary, but highly publicized and dramatized, environmental pollution. In the long run the pollution is mitigated by human and natural processes. We have seen the immediate effects of the Exxon Valdez oil spill (1989), and the horrific BP Deep Water Horizon platform explosion and oil spill (2010). But given the fact that this industry operates 24 hours a day, 365 days of every year, providing excellent, efficient, and affordable energy that drives our economy and quality of life, the overall record of safety, productivity and benefit to humanity is invaluable and underrated.

The industry that explores, extracts, and refines oil and gas is not given the credit that it deserves for the innovation, the efficiency and affordability of the products that make our lives immeasurably better. The oil industry makes so many by-products from every barrel of oil, that they waste almost none of the raw material.

In addition to the basic energy needs for transportation and electricity, here are some of the products that are made from oil and its by-products: Lipstick, Make-up, Nail polish, Purses, Shoes, Panty hose, Hair color, Shampoo, Toothbrush, Refrigerators, Luggage, Eye glasses, Contact lenses, Sun glasses, Electric blankets, Surf boards,

Motorcycle helmets, Tires, Fishing lures, Golf bags, Basketballs, Deodorant, Life jackets, Car batteries, Toilet seats, Fishing rods, Shower curtains, Guitar string, CD's, Computer keyboards, Artificial turf, Dice, Ice chests, Parachutes, Pillows, Golf balls, Plastic, Asphalt, Synthetic rubber, Wax, Fertilizer, Pesticides, Detergent, Packaging materials, Paint, Antiseptics, Soap, Antihistamines, Food preservatives, Umbrellas, Trash bags, Water pipes, Anti-freeze, Crayons, Aspirin, and about 5,944 other products and raw materials.

Common sense tells us that fossil fuels might be a finite resource. In 1977, then President Jimmy Carter made the prediction that the world would run out of oil within 35 years (by 2012). Typical liberal point of view (no offense intended), but President Carter ignored the key factor of *free market innovation*. As conventional oil reserves depleted and market prices increased, "Enhanced Oil Recovery (EOR)" technologies were developed by the U.S. oil and gas industry, that have made un-conventional oil reserves *which vastly exceed conventional reserves*, accessible.

Furthermore, there are new technologies under research and development that could be used to extend the life of old oil fields and gain access to so-called unconventional petroleum reserves like oil sands. Innovation in the free market never stops. The oil industry has been highly successful with game-changing innovation in its history. The U.S. has gone from being oil dependent on imported oil, to being the world's largest producer of oil. And who knows, Jimmy Carter, what new future innovations will come about to extend the life and efficiency of the current resources, and even minimize the environmental impacts as we currently know them to be? If we have learned anything from history, it is, "to never say never".

Now let me speak to the people who read this and say, "no way dude, you are just wrong man...oil is bad and you are polluting the environment and hurting the climate!" I know you are out there. Here is the reality: at this point in time we do not have a viable, affordable, and sufficiently scalable source of alternative energy to replace oil and gas. We just don't!

Here are the current energy uses:

Petroleum – 36.4%

Natural Gas – 29%

Coal - 16.4%

Nuclear – 8.5%

Biomass – 4.8%

Hydroelectric – 2.5%

Solar (1.9%) & Wind (0.5%) – 2.4%

The current renewable energy industry is a worthy effort, but it is in its infancy, and is woefully insufficient to meet the worlds energy needs. The solar panels cannot produce enough energy to be a viable alternative to natural gas or even coal. The battery technology is insufficient to store backup energy for the night time or for cloudy days. The wind farms are even less productive than the solar panel arrays. You can't build enough wind turbines. And some days the wind doesn't blow. What then?

Tesla is manufacturing all electric cars. There are currently two models of Tesla, and the sale price ranges from about

$85,000 to $140,000 depending on the model you select and the options that you choose to add. These electric cars have a range of about 250 miles, when you factor in the use of air conditioning or heat to control the interior climate of the vehicle, depending on the weather. A full charge of the car's battery takes from six to eight hours with a standard wall charging unit. If you can reach a Tesla charging station the charge only takes about one hour. According to the Tesla website, assuming $2.70 per gallon cost of gasoline, the electric charge is about 50% savings vs. the cost of gasoline. Given the capital cost of this technology (the car), the average driver cannot afford the Tesla. Furthermore, with the current state of the battery technology, the range is limited and the charge time excessive, making the Tesla a very costly and relatively inconvenient alternative to gasoline engine cars.

Tesla Motors has not been able to achieve any financial success. Tesla's balance sheet at December 31, 2016 indicates "shareholders equity" (the amount by which assets exceed liabilities) totaling $4.7 billion, however that includes $7.7 billion in "Additional Paid In Capital", which is money raised from shareholders. So without the additional capital raised from the market, Tesla has a significant negative net worth, and would not have cash to operate the company. The actual operating losses of Tesla's operations total <$3 billion>. Tesla has to keep raising new capital to cover its operating losses in order to have enough cash to keep producing and selling the electric cars while trying the develop the technology to become economically self-sufficient. The question is, can Tesla keep raising capital to cover its operating losses? Tesla lost $890 million in 2015 and lost $770 million in 2016.

Tesla acquired Elon Musk's (the founder of Tesla Motors) solar power company "SolarCity Corporation". SolarCity manufactures solar panels, and has developed a new product, which is solar roofing tiles, that are designed to be used in lieu of standard roofing shingles. SolarCity is estimated to produce about 25 percent of the national solar panel business. Like Tesla Motors, SolarCity has struggled to make money while developing the solar technology.

The State of New York built a new factory for SolarCity at a cost of $750 million, paid by the New York tax payers. The factory in Buffalo is to be leased by SolarCity for $1 per year, and is projected to provide nearly 2,000 jobs when production is at full capacity. But that assumes the product is in demand. The factory was completed and handed over to SolarCity in the summer of 2016, however no jobs have been created yet and no product manufacturing has commenced. SolarCity estimates that the new factory will not open and commence operations until late 2017 or even later in 2018, due to problems with the technology development.

Meanwhile, SolarCity's acquisition by Tesla is essentially a bailout for SolarCity, which has lost over $2 billion in five years (2011-2015). The company has $3 billion in debt. These two companies are struggling to reach the break-even point despite the fact that Elon Musk has received nearly $5 billion in government grants, tax breaks, discounted loans, environmental credits, and the new factory in Buffalo, New York, for Tesla, SolarCity and Musk's private company known as SpaceX.

The purpose of this information is not to disparage Elon Musk, or any of his struggling companies. It is to highlight the point that I made earlier which is that at this time in history there is no reliable, scalable and affordable alternative source of energy to replace the plentiful, affordable and totally reliable fossil fuels. Fossil fuels are a blessing from God and they provide the wonderful standard of living that we enjoy.

I know. You might be saying, well you are just a "negative Nelly", Mr. Oil man! To that I say, just be patient. Innovation will provide the answer some day. Let me remind you, that in the 1960s a single computer filled an entire room. And then someone invented the microchip, and the integrated circuit. And the rest, as they say, "is history". Some innovation of that nature is certainly possible for Solar energy. I'm not sure about wind, but time will tell.

As mad as you are at me right now, I will make you a promise. There will come a time, sometime in the future, when some inventor in the free market will discover a new technology, or a new source of energy, maybe it will even be something from outer space or another world, that will eventually make fossil fuels obsolete. It is inevitable. That is how dynamic the American free market economy is. Whole industries will spring up to support the development of that new energy resource. And when they do Exxon-Mobil and all of their competitors will be in the game. The oil industry is not in business to make oil. They are in the business to make money! And they are very good at it.

In the last 50 years, we have seen the advent of the personal computer, the internet and email. Forty years ago, we didn't have mobile phones, and we could only watch three television channels, with rabbit ears, on crappy TVs that weighed 300 pounds! It was just ten years ago that Apple gave us the game changing and wonderful iPhone!

Innovation is the solution to every problem of mankind. Innovation will not be provided by the government, or the ridiculous UN. The motive for profit and the will to risk venture capital is the driving force behind this most magnificent incubator of invention that we call the American free market economy.

In this lies your hope, if you are one that is not buying my "earth's HVAC system" anecdote.

Luke 12:24

Look at the birds. They don't plant or harvest, they don't have storerooms or barns, but God feeds them. And you are worth much more than birds.

Just as sure as I am that God provided the resources that we are using today, and that mankind eventually through time, exploration and innovation, was able to find and develop these resources to make life on earth better, I am equally sure that there are even greater and more abundant resources for our future, that right now just exceed our current imagination and technology. But in time, mankind will find and innovate the energy of the future.

Until then drive your car, fly on your jet, charge up your Tesla, keep your house cool in the summer and warm in the winter. We have plenty of oil and gas, and coal, and there is no global warming climate crisis.

Chapter Seven

The Hoax

They can't prove it, because "it" does not exist. Global warming is a hoax.

Back in chapter one we discussed that the UN IPCC gets the global temperature data used in the climate models to support the theory of anthropogenic global warming, from NOAA, NASA, and the Climatic Research Unit (University of East Anglia, UK).

The Climatic Research Unit (the "CRU") is self-proclaimed as "one of the world's leading institutions concerned with the study of natural and anthropogenic climate change". The

CRU has a staff of approximately twenty research scientists and students, and it has developed a number of the "data sets" widely used in climate research, including the global temperature record used to monitor the state of the climate system, as well as statistical software packages and climate models. The CRU is a significant contributor of historical temperature, and other climate data that is used in the IPCC climate models. Those climate models are the source of the information behind the opinions held by the UN, the EPA, Al Gore, Barack Obama, foreign leaders, and many famous people in pop culture, in the media and in the academic world, that there is allegedly global warming that is causing damage to the planet, and that the warming is caused by human actions. (blah-blah-blah)

In November 2009, a collection of email messages and data files were "leaked" from the CRU, apparently by a disgruntled whistleblower. The identity of the whistleblower has not yet been disclosed. The purpose of the leak was apparently to reveal to the public a scandal within the CRU, involving scientific fraud and data manipulation in support of the theory of alleged anthropogenic global warming. The leak included more than a thousand emails that had been exchanged between the scientists within the CRU. These email messages provided evidence of fraud and deceit by the climate scientists.

The scandal called "Climategate" is broadly regarded as having unmasked the biggest scientific hoax in modern world history. The Climategate emails and data files severely damaged the credibility of the CRU's assumptions and climate model output, that is the basis for the CRU's opinion regarding anthropogenic global warming.

The leaked email messages and data files revealed three shocking and corrupt offenses by the scientists of the CRU: (1) fraud; (2) deceit; and (3) a cover-up. The **fraud** was the manipulation of the data by the scientists using their climate models to arrive at a pre-determined outcome. The scientists manipulated the data by using lower distant historical temperatures, and adjusting the more recent temperatures upwards, to give the illusion that the global warming has been accelerating as the CO_2 emissions increased in modern times. The existence of the data manipulation results in all the prior climate modeling by the

CRU, and the opinions that were produced by the models to be judged to be a complete hoax. It also means that the entirety of the billions of dollars invested by the United States government with the UN in climate research, was completely wasted.

The **deceit** consisted of the CRU scientists taking actions to silence any of their peers who questioned the findings of the CRU climate models, by refusing to disclose any conflicting assumptions and data, and by refusing to recognize any scientific journal which agreed to publish the work of any of their critics. The emails revealed that a number of scientists were discussing schemes intended to suppress the scientific peer review process, in order to prevent access to publication for dissenting articles.

The **cover-up** was a conspiracy in which the scientists employed devious tactics over a period of years that allowed the CRU to avoid releasing any of their data to outsiders, including a tacit denial in response to requests under the UK freedom of information laws.

The Climategate emails indicated that the fraud, deceit, and cover-up also extended to the United States. The scandal revealed that all the data centers which included NOAA and NASA had conspired to manipulate the global temperature records in order to indicate that global temperatures had risen faster in the 20th century than they actually had, to fit the narrative of anthropogenic global warming.

The Climategate emails revealed that NASA had systematically eliminated 75% of their global stations for collecting temperature data in their climate models, with an apparent bias toward limiting the high latitude and higher altitude stations. The number of weather stations used to collect temperature data had been reduced from approximately 6,600 to approximately 1,550. The temperature data for the stations that were eliminated from the larger population was extrapolated from temperature data in other cities in their "general geographic" region. The selection of the remaining station locations slanted NASA's data and climate change conclusions to advance the preferred global warming agenda instead of including the total amount of factual data in an unbiased scientific analysis.

The damage that was done by the Climategate scandal essentially killed the United Nations sponsored Copenhagen Climate Conference in December 2009. The 2009 calendar had begun as a year of so much hope and anticipation by the global warming activists, both domestically and internationally. Gone was the Bush administration that had refused to recognize the 1997 Kyoto Protocol. Now they had a new Democrat controlled Congress, and President Obama with his hugely progressive liberal agenda. Their plan was to enact global warming legislation and sign a new global warming treaty. And then, just when they thought they had victory in their grasp, the Climategate bomb dropped. The credibility of the global warming science of the UN IPCC was tainted.

Copenhagen had been planned to be the conference where a set of stringent, verifiable, binding and internationally enforceable greenhouse gas emissions targets would be agreed upon. There were some preliminary discussions of requiring as much as 30 percent cuts in CO_2 emissions by 2020 for developed nations. Some hoped that developing nations such as China and India would surrender their exemptions from the Kyoto Protocol. But none of those things happened.

All that was left after two weeks of meetings, fine wine and fine dining, photo ops and press conferences was a vague agreement that essentially said that it would be nice if each nation would go ahead and try to reduce CO2 emissions, on their own. China and other developing nations did not want the language to have even a hint that they might be obligated to do something to reduce CO2 emissions. Non-binding promises from developed nations to provide finance to poor nations were also completely meaningless. The reality is that restrictions on energy use in the name of "fighting global warming" are a costly, economically devastating, and ineffective solution to a non-existent threat.

The Copenhagen Agreement accomplished absolutely nothing. Copenhagen was emblematic of the eight years of the Obama Presidency. It made a lot of noise. It stirred up a lot of conflict. It spent a ton of money. But it got nothing meaningful done.

Have you ever heard of the "hockey stick graph"? This is another fine example of a biased scientist manipulating the data, to get to the desired conclusion. I am not going to go into discussions of the names of the scientists, because to me they aren't important. They all fall together into a big bucket of scientists who are part of the fanatical group that promotes the theory of global warming, and they blame human activities for the so-called warming. (insert "eye roll", here)

The "hockey stick" is a graph that presents an illustration of historic temperature data. It depicts a period of time from 1000 AD to 2000 AD. The global average temperature is shown to be gently declining from 1000 AD until about 1900 AD, when suddenly the temperatures begin to climb, and they steadily climb to a level that is far above where they had previously been in the prior millennium. The shape of the graph is the long shaft of the hockey stick (the allegedly declining temperatures from 1000-1900 AD) with the blade of the hockey stick at the end (the sharply increasing temperatures from 1900 AD to the present).

This hockey stick graph and the temperature data that it is based on is the propaganda that fueled the claims that President Obama kept making, basically every year from

2009 through 2015, alleging that each year had been the hottest on the global temperature record. We now know that was not true.

What the scientist did was to go back and change (manipulate) the historical global average temperatures to make it appear as if there was a nice gentle linear decline from 1000 to 1900 AD. Then the temperature slope goes on a sudden linear upward slope throughout the 20th century.

Why? Well, because mankind was selfishly developing lots of great stuff during the industrial revolution and beyond to make our lives better, like cars and trucks (and SUVs), ships, trains and airplanes, electric power plants, factories and petrochemical plants. And they were all powered by fossil fuels! Gas, oil and coal ("evil" coal). The carbon dioxide was just pumping into the atmosphere in higher amounts, year after year!

Here's the problem for the hockey stick scientists. The historical record of the temperatures from 1000 AD to 1350 AD encompasses the "Medieval Warm Period", when the global temperature was warmer than it is today. That spike in the global temperature does not match the smooth linear decline (cooling) that is depicted in the hockey stick graph from 1000 AD to 1400 AD. After the Little Ice Age cooling period of roughly 1500 to 1650 AD, there was a warming period from 1650 to 1700. That also does not match the smooth linear decline that is depicted in the hockey stick graph from 1600 to 1900 AD.

During the time segment from 1000 AD to 1800 AD there was a period of significant warming (warmer than we are today), then cooling, and then warming again. These climate cycles all occurred long before mankind was emitting any CO_2 into the atmosphere from the use of fossil fuels. The earth's temperature was naturally changing because of the inherent forces within the earth's climate, and forces acting upon the planet from the solar system. Those same forces within the planet's climate system and the solar system are at work, and affecting the earth's climate today. There has been mild warming of 1.5 degrees Fahrenheit overall from 1850 to 1997. Since 1997 there has been no further change of the global average surface temperature. The "Pause".

The warming has stopped for now 20 years, despite the fact that carbon dioxide emissions have continued to increase world-wide due to the modernization of developing countries. This leads to the obvious conclusion that the variation in the global average temperature is not related exclusively to the CO2 emissions. The temperature variance is being caused by the earth's God given natural processes over which mankind has absolutely no control. Those natural processes are more powerful, and as such they counter-act the greenhouse gas effect.

That is the climate conclusion that the scientists behind the global warming theory, who are working for the UN IPCC, simply cannot abide. This is the reason why they manipulated the data that caused their climate models to produce the outcome to falsely illustrate the theory that global warming is being caused by humans. It is just that simple. And shameful. And they really thought that they could get away with it, because they control the narrative with liberal ideology in the UN, the liberal governments of the member nations and the progressive liberal media.

For the scientists to go back and attempt to revise the historical temperatures is an act of deceit and utter desperation. You can't revise history! History is in the books, and the revisionist scientists have been revealed as liars.

In the decade of the 1970s global cooling fears were widespread among many scientists and in the media. Back then there was no UN IPCC to promote global cooling. There was no federal government funding of billions of dollars, like there is today to promote man-made global warming. The fears of a "coming ice age" appeared in scientific literature, at scientific conferences, in the media and was discussed by prominent scientists in academia.

In the April 28, 1975 issue of Newsweek magazine, there was an article titled "The Cooling World". Following is an excerpt from this article:

"The evidence in support of these predictions has now begun to accumulate so massively that meteorologists are hard-pressed to keep up with it. In England, farmers have seen their growing season decline by about two weeks since 1950, with a resultant overall loss in grain production estimated at up to 100,000 tons annually. The central fact is

that after three quarters of a century of extraordinarily mild conditions, the earth's climate seems to be cooling down. Meteorologists disagree about the cause and extent of the cooling trend, as well as over its specific impact on local weather conditions. But they are almost unanimous in the view that the trend will reduce agricultural productivity for the rest of the century. If the climatic change is as profound as some of the pessimist's fear, the resulting famines could be catastrophic. "A major climatic change would force economic and social adjustments on a worldwide scale," warns a recent report by the National Academy of Sciences, "because the global patterns of food production and population that have evolved are implicitly dependent on the climate of the present century." Climatologists are pessimistic that political leaders will take any positive action to compensate for the climatic change, or even to allay its effects."

There you have it, straight from the pages of Newsweek in 1975. There was documented global cooling from 1940 through 1970. This period of global temperature cooling occurred during a time when the emissions of CO_2 from the use of fossil fuels was growing substantially around the world. Yet the hockey stick scientists continued to promote their narrative that there was uninterrupted cooling from 1000 AD until 1900 AD, and then thereafter was a consistent and linear growth line of the global temperature. The growth of the global temperature was of course attributed directly to human emissions of CO_2. We know that there is significant evidence, which I have presented in chapter six of this book, that indicates that the volume of CO_2 in the atmosphere is not the singular influence on the global temperature of the earth.

Despite all of the bad press from the disastrous 2009 Copenhagen climate summit and the damage to the credibility of the UN IPCC caused by the Climategate emails, the global warming activists never stopped advocating for their cause. With the liberal and progressive Barack Obama as President of the United States, the scientists continued to receive significant political support, as well as the all-important research grants from the Obama administration. The United Nations planned another climate summit for the negotiations of a global treaty to reduce carbon dioxide emissions worldwide, prior to the end of President Obama's second term in office. The Paris Climate Accord was a conference of the member nations of the UN IPCC that took place from November 30 – December 12, 2015.

The global warming scientists had a problem that they needed to solve before the Paris conference. UN scientists had conceded in 2013 that there indeed has been a pause in the warming of the global average temperature. There had been no further warming since 1997. This fact added credibility to the theory that CO_2 emissions do not exclusively impact the global temperature, because there are natural processes of the earth's climate, that are outside of mankind's control or influence, that are more powerful than the atmospheric greenhouse effect, and are in fact what balances global climate variability.

In June 2015 NOAA (the U.S. National Oceanic and Atmospheric Administration) published an astonishing report that stated that the so-called "pause" in global warming had in fact never existed, and that global temperatures had been rising from 1997 through 2014. The report which became known as "the Pausebuster paper", was enthusiastically reported by the mainstream media with a virtual public relations fanfare. NOAA published the Pausebuster paper with the intent of having an impact on the world leaders who would be their Nation's decision makers at the Paris Climate conference in December 2015.

The 195 member-nations reached an agreement during the Paris climate conference within the United Nations Framework Convention on Climate Change (UNFCCC) to deal with greenhouse gas emissions mitigation, adaptation and finance starting in the year 2020. The agreement included five commitments: (1) Nations will collectively attempt to hold the increase in the global average temperature to 2 degrees Celsius (3.6 degrees Fahrenheit) above pre-industrial levels, by 2100; (2) "Peak" (cap) global greenhouse gas emissions by the year 2050; (3) Developed Nations will fund $100 billion annually to assist developing nations to become more "sustainable". (4) "Stock-take" in 2023, and every 5 years thereafter – which means each nation is expected to evaluate the implementation of the Agreement (self-compliance); (5) There will be no outside agency to verify emission levels for each nation, however there is a framework for transparency to report progress and compliance (a "non-binding" agreement).

The economic costs of the implementation of the Paris climate agreement would be devastating to the United States economy, and crippling to many U.S. workers. Companies would have to pass higher costs on to consumers, or absorb the costs which would prevent hiring and new capital investment. As prices rise, consumers buy less, and companies will drop employees, reduce operations, or move to other countries where the cost of doing business is lower. The result would be economic chaos with fewer opportunities for American employees, lower incomes, less economic growth, and higher unemployment. Furthermore, the United States government would likely be tasked with funding the majority of the $100 billion annual developing nations assistance fund, because the U.S. is considered the most developed nation, and is also blamed for causing a large proportionate share of the CO_2 emissions in the atmosphere to date.

In February 2017, a high-level whistleblower revealed that NOAA defied internal policy rules for scientific integrity in the process of producing the false and misleading Pausebuster paper. The whistleblower was confirmed to be a top NOAA scientist with a sterling reputation. NOAA scientists used misleading and unverified data that was never subjected to NOAA's internal evaluation process. The whistleblower had objected to the publication of the false and misleading data in the report in 2015, but he was overruled by his NOAA superiors. The Paris conference representatives were misled by the fraudulent NOAA Pausebuster paper as they negotiated the Paris Agreement, which committed the United States to unnecessary reductions in the use of fossil fuels (the back bone of our economy) and committed the United States to funding billions of tax payer dollars to developing nations for the fraud of "climate sustainability".

The basis of the NOAA Pausebuster paper was two "new" sets of temperature data. One set was land based temperature readings, and the other was from the surface of the oceans. The ocean data used methodology known to be unreliable, which overstated the warming, which of course was the scientists desired outcome! The scientists eliminated data that was obtained from floating buoys, which is the most reliable method for ocean temperature collection, and replaced it with data obtained from ocean going ships. The readings from ships are known to be inaccurate, because the ship itself is a source of heat, and the depth of the water intake on the ship varies based on the load being carried by the ship. The scientists knew that they would get higher temperature data from the ships dataset. That was an outright fraud.

The land temperature data was determined by a new version of NOAA's land records, allegedly obtained from about 4,000 weather stations around the globe. This new version of the land temperature data indicated cooler temperatures in the past, and higher recent temperature readings. This made the global warming look steeper, and eliminated the pause (since 1997). Again, the desired outcome for the NOAA scientists.

The whistleblower revealed that the scientists had failed to follow any of the formal NOAA procedures normally followed to approve and archive data. The scientists also used an experimental early-run of a climate program that was supposed to combine two previously separate sets of records. There were large unexplained adjustments to the raw temperature data. Similar to the previously discussed hockey stick graph scandal, the scientists managed to produce revised temperature data that supports a politically predetermined conclusion in favor of the theory of human caused global warming. What a surprise!

Later the whistleblower confronted the scientists about the data. He was then told that the computer that was used to process the data had completely crashed. As a result, the data supporting the Pausebuster paper can never be reproduced or verified. Some NOAA scientists had engaged in a coverup when they were called to task by the whistleblower. In the light of day, the Pausebuster paper was a complete fraud that was used to influence the outcome of the Paris climate conference.

On June 1, 2017 President Trump announced that the United States will withdraw from the Paris Climate Accord. President Trump had the option of withdrawing from the treaty because former President Obama never submitted the Paris climate agreement to Congress for ratification. President Trump correctly stated that the Paris Agreement imposed unfair environmental standards on American businesses and workers. He vowed to stand with the people of the United States against what he called a "draconian" international deal.

President Trump said that he would be willing to negotiate a better deal for the United States, and the administration said he had placed calls to the leaders of Britain, France, Germany, and Canada to personally explain his decision. The leaders of France, Germany and Italy issued a joint statement saying that the Paris climate accord was "irreversible" and could not be renegotiated. That is a typical response from the liberal left. Whether it is domestic or international, liberals are unwilling to compromise, and that is the biggest problem in the political culture of our time. The foolish and politically correct European countries will cripple their economies in the name of a non-existent climate issue.

We have discussed three significant scandals in this chapter that have occurred since 2009 (during the Obama Presidency) in which scientists who favor the anthropogenic global warming theory have engaged in literal fraud: (1) the Climategate email scandal; (2) the hockey stick graph data scandal; and (3) the Pausebuster paper scandal. In all three scandals, the scientists were caught manipulating temperature data to make it appear that there is significant global warming. But in fact, there is only mild climate variability caused by the earth's natural processes, which mankind cannot control and over which mankind has no influence whatsoever.

Anthropogenic global warming is a religion that exists only in the hearts and minds of the faithful activists, and in the climate models that their scientists create. Just consider the facts. The global warming alarmists base their concerns on predictions of future events to be caused by alleged rising temperatures. These rising temperatures are not based on current events, but on the predictions produced by the climate models. The same models (by the way) that scientists have been caught manipulating the data and assumptions for. Again, going back to the facts, the global warming alarmists have repeatedly predicted climatic calamities for the last 30 years, including: coastal flooding to be caused by rising sea levels; complete melting of the Arctic sea ice; increases in drought frequency; increases in powerful hurricane frequency; rising temperatures correlating with the growth in global CO2 emissions.

Not one of these predictions have actually occurred, nor has there even been a developing trend aside from the normal historical variations, to be concerned about. Anthropogenic global warming exists only in the abstract, and in the climate models of biased (and some corrupt) scientists.

Now, I want to explain to you what I think the global warming science hoax is really all about. Global warming is not about the climate. Global warming is not about science either. Global warming, or militant environmentalism is about the agenda of the leftist activists internationally, and the radical left of the Democrat party in the U.S., to control the destiny of the American people. It is about power, influence, and money. If you don't have the ability to invent a great product, and build a great company, the best source of huge amounts of money and power is in national politics. The United States government spends $4 trillion per year. Now that is some power right there, people! If your political party gets control of that budget, and you are in a position of leadership, then man, you have power! And power is money in Washington DC.

Now get your tin foil conspiracy hat back out, and put it on, because this is a little heavy but it is true. When the Berlin Wall fell (1989), and then the Soviet Union collapsed (1991), and communism had truly failed, the far-left loonies needed a new political cause to embrace. Militant environmentalism was born. You see, the one thing that the far-left loonies really oppose is capitalism. That is why they loved socialism and communism. But when those economic systems failed dramatically, they found an even better cause to promote. Better, because there is a greater opportunity for control over vast amounts of money and political power in the United States.

Now that brings us to the global warming scientists, and why they do the things that they do, such as committing fraud and manipulating temperature data to create the outcome that supports their completely bogus theory of anthropogenic global warming. Many of these scientists are working for government agencies like NOAA, NASA, the

EPA, and the Department of Energy. Government funding of climate research is very biased toward work that concludes that global warming is a threat to the environment. So, if you work for these agencies and you want to keep your job, well you better toe the "company line", or you won't be around for long.

The largest supporter of environmental groups and climate researchers is the United States government, through research grants. The U.S. government throughout the Obama administration was funding about $80 billion dollars per year toward UN sponsored climate science research projects, through various U.S. agency budgets. In addition to the UN research, the federal government also funds over $100 million per year to various domestic environmental lobbying groups. Now, get this. Those environmental lobbying groups have lobbyists who, you guessed it, lobby the U.S. government to support environmental causes. It's a money and power merry go-round that you the American tax payer are funding year after fiscal year.

The environmental movement in the United States is a massive financial enterprise with a lot of money and power, and it is funded primarily by our government. Those who work in this enterprise do not want the merry go-round to stop, so it is in their best interest to keep the environmental and climate scare stories coming. No one in this climate party wants to hear, "hey don't worry, global warming isn't really a problem...the scientists were all wrong!".

Notwithstanding what the activists don't want to hear, the earth's climate system is NOT fragile. Human activities that are making life better for all people of the world are NOT harming the climate. The climate has its own internal mechanisms that are far beyond mankind's control, that were ordained by God almighty, and that are maintaining the climate just as they have been since the dawn of time.

There have been five ice ages in the 4.5 billion-year history of the earth. Within the ice ages, there are periods of extensive glacier coverage (known as "glacial periods") as well as warmer climate times that are known as "interglacial periods". The Earth is currently in an interglacial period of the "Quaternary Ice Age", known as the "Holocene Period". The Quaternary Ice Age consists of the last 1.8 million years. The Holocene (the current warm period) started about 11,500 years ago.

In the relative "recent" history of earth, during the time of civilized man there have been some dramatic shifts in the earth's climate. From approximately 1050 to 1350 AD the period was known as the "Medieval Warm Period" when the climate was actually warmer than it is today, and there were no cars, trucks, trains, or coal fired power plants belching CO_2 into the atmosphere. The Medieval warm period was followed by the "Little Ice Age" from 1400 to about 1850 AD, when the global temperatures were about two degrees cooler than today.

According to the anthropogenic global warming activists, it is the increase in CO_2 caused by human activities in the last 100 years that is the primary cause of the phantom global warming that hasn't really happened yet, but their climate models keep predicting that it is coming in a big way. They say the climate will be cooking by 2100. However, the earth has managed to start and end four massive ice ages that lasted tens of millions of years each over the last 2.4 billion years, all before there was any human existence on the planet. Doesn't that give you some perspective on just how small and insignificant mankind actually is in comparison to the existence of the planet?

How did those four ice ages start and then end with no help from mankind? God's hand of creation was at work. There are three very powerful forces of the solar system that are at work on our planet. These forces are in a constant cycle that never stops, and they are of such power and force that modern man has no ability to influence them in any way.

The first very powerful force is known as the earth's "Precession". This is the pointing of the earth's axis, or a more-simple explanation is the earth's "wobble", like a spinning top will wobble when it slows down. The earth will rotate (wobble around) 360 degrees on its axis over a time period of about 23,000 years. This affects the intensity and distribution of the sun to the northern hemisphere. This is very important because most land masses are in the northern hemisphere, and the northern hemisphere is where the growth and advancement of glaciers always begins.

The second very powerful force is known as the "Obliquity", or the degree of "tilt" of the earth's axis. Low obliquity means less sunlight in the northern hemisphere, which will cause the advancement of glaciers. The earth is currently at 23.5 degrees of tilt, which is a good level of tilt for the sun's exposure to the northern hemisphere. However, the obliquity is in a decreasing trend. This trend will bottom out about 12,000 years from now, and when that happens a colder climate will most likely commence a glacial advancement period. We won't be here to see it.

The third very powerful force is known as the "Eccentricity" of the earth's orbit. In a cycle of about 100,000 years the earth's orbit around the sun will go from a nice normal circle, to an elongated elliptical. We are currently in a circle orbit, which is good for a warm climate. This is the longest cycle of the three planetary forces. Eccentricity won't have a changing impact on the climate during our relatively brief lives, but it certainly is an explanation for the beginning and end of the prior ice ages in the planet's history.

Let's go back to the global warming alarmist's theory of anthropogenic global warming. The greenhouse gases are an important tool in helping the earth to keep the surface of the planet sufficiently warm for plants, creatures and humans to live. However, the greenhouse gases consist primarily of water vapor (80%). Carbon dioxide only makes up about 10%, and the other 10% includes methane, ozone, and some others. It is very important to understand that the warming effect of carbon dioxide does NOT have a linear relationship with the volume of carbon dioxide in the atmosphere. In other words, 2 times the CO_2 does NOT equal 2 times the warming of the greenhouse blanket. It's not even close.

The naturally occurring greenhouse gases in the earth's atmosphere make the planet's surface 30 degrees Celsius warmer than the planet would be without them in the atmosphere. That makes the average global temperature 15 degrees Celsius instead of -15 degrees Celsius (15 degrees C = 59 degrees Fahrenheit). Before the industrial revolution the carbon dioxide in the atmosphere was 286 parts per million, so the carbon dioxide component was contributing about 3 degrees Celsius to the warming of the planet's surface (10% of the greenhouse gas effect). The relationship between the ongoing growth of carbon dioxide in the atmosphere and the change of the global average temperature has a declining effect because of the saturation nature of carbon dioxide. The counter-acting effect of numerous natural forces in the earth's climate (example: clouds and precipitation) also overwhelmingly balance the effect of the growth of the CO_2 in the atmosphere. We know that there has been no increase in the global average temperature for the last 20 years, despite the fact that CO_2 emissions worldwide have continued to increase due to the growth of developing nations around the globe.

The inescapable truth of the earth's power and adaptability has so frustrated the global warming scientists that they have stooped to cheating and manipulation to try to change the facts, and their fraud has been exposed.

Who and what would you rather trust in this debate? A sovereign and all-knowing God, the creator of the Universe, for whom our forefathers fought tyranny and waged a revolutionary war for the freedom to worship? Or a bunch of biased and corrupt scientists and government bureaucrats who are making their living by taxing your income, and who want to tax you even more just because you put gas in your car, cool your home in the summer and warm it in the winter, and live your life in liberty as is granted by the constitution?

"By wisdom the Lord laid the earth's foundations, by understanding he set the heavens in place; By his knowledge the deeps were divided, and the clouds let drop the dew." -- **Proverbs 3: 19-20**

This is an easy decision for me.

Chapter Eight

Al Gore – The Snake Oil Salesman

Al Gore is the leader of the radical extremist global warming movement and he has made the signature influence in shaping the opinion of pop culture stars regarding global warming. He has been an environmental activist since the early 1980s, and has written several books on the subject of global warming. Al Gore also put together a documentary slide show presenting his ideology about global warming.

I have dubbed Gore as "The Snake Oil Salesman". The phrase conjures up images of seedy profiteers of the early 20th century carnivals and traveling shows, exploiting the fearful and unsuspecting public by selling tonics that promised to cure a wide variety of ailments including chronic pain, headaches, and kidney trouble. In time all of these false "cures" were exposed to be a quack remedy or panacea, and a total and complete fraud.

What is even worse about the snake oil salesman Al Gore is that not only is the "cure" that he is selling (mandatory reduction in the use of fossil fuels) a total fraud, but the alleged ailment (man-made global warming) is equally a hoax!

After his loss in the 2000 Presidential election, Gore began to focus his efforts to broadly communicate his message regarding global warming. He traveled the United States, and internationally, presenting his Power Point slide show to lecture halls of university students, political groups and to politicians. Al Gore was also invited to make his presentation to members of the Hollywood elite.

After a presentation in Hollywood, Gore was approached by Laurie David, the wife of Larry David the co-creator of "Seinfeld", to produce his slideshow documentary as a motion picture for the big screen. By doing so he could reach a wider audience. Laurie David is referred to as the "priestess of Hollywood activism", as she is likely second only to Al Gore in environmental publicity efforts. She has been quoted as saying, *"helping to bring Al Gore's keynote on global warming to a "theater near you" has been the highlight of my career"*. Well, congratulations Laurie, you have been conned by "The Snake Oil Salesman".

Gore did get his "keynote on global warming" produced as a big screen movie in 2006, titled "An Inconvenient Truth". It is a one hour & thirty-six minute production that made quite a lot of revenue. According to public sources, An Inconvenient Truth generated $52.7 million from the box office (U.S. and international), and another $31.6 million from DVD sales.

The movie "An Inconvenient Truth" begins with Al Gore standing on the stage of a lecture hall, with an audience of about 350-400 people. Behind him is a very large video screen for the slides and videos that he uses to illustrate his narrative. As he walks on to the stage, he says to the audience, *"I am Al Gore, and I used to be the next President of the United States of America"*. The crowd laughs, as Gore responds, "*I don't find that particularly funny*", and then he smiles and the crowd laughs again.

The movie then cuts away from the lecture hall scene, and Gore narrates by saying, "*I've been trying to tell this story for a long time, and I feel as if I've failed to get the message across*", meanwhile you are shown some very dramatic scenes of video including some Arctic sea ice sparsely floating in the Arctic Ocean, a parched desert, a petrochemical plant with steam belching from an exhaust tower. Ominous music is playing in the background. Then, you are shown a satellite image of hurricane Katrina, followed by very dramatic video of the hurricane making landfall and inflicting damage on the City of New Orleans. In the background of this scene of destruction is the voice of former Mayor Ray Nagin pleading for help on the radio, and blaming anyone except his office, for the victims who are stranded in the city by the flooding (the same Ray Nagin who is now serving a 10-year sentence in federal prison after being convicted for bribery and fraud while serving as New Orleans Mayor).

Gore then makes the statement that *"there are good people, who are in politics in both parties, who hold this at arms-length because if they acknowledge it and recognize it then the moral imperative to make big changes is inescapable"*. Gore is referencing the subject of global warming. Obviously, the "moral imperative" as he puts it, is his very biased opinion.

The movie then returns to the original scene of the lecture hall, with Gore speaking to the audience. He tells the audience and he illustrates with photos of the earth taken from outer space, that the earth's atmosphere is the most "vulnerable part" of the earth's ecological system because it is so thin in comparison to the earth itself. Note: just ask the NASA engineers who are responsible for designing the heat shields that protect the space craft upon re-entry, how "thin and vulnerable" the earth's atmosphere is! The atmosphere that protects the earth from the vacuum of outer space is actually quite robust.

Gore goes on to say that this thin layer of atmosphere is being "thickened" by all of the "global warming pollution" that is being "put up there", while on the screen behind him the audience is being shown more images of factories and petroleum plants with smoke and steam coming out of big exhaust towers. He then says that with the thickening of the atmosphere, more of the "reflected infrared" energy (from the sun) is trapped, and so the atmosphere heats up worldwide..."*that's global warming*" he says with emphasis.

Note: he never gives any actual temperature data to back up his opinion that the atmosphere heats up worldwide, but I digress.

Gore then says, "*this is the traditional description of global warming, but I have a better illustration*". He then plays a humorous cartoon that shows a comical "Mr. Sun Ray" coming to earth and then turning to go back to outer space. But then several mean looking greenhouse gas "gangsters" beat up Mr. Sun Ray and he falls back to earth. The greenhouse gas gangsters are fiendishly laughing, surrounding the earth and holding brief cases full of cash. At the end of the cartoon, there is light laughter from the audience, followed by applause. Very silly, but it furthers the point that Gore is making about CO_2 being the direct cause of the alleged global warming.

Up to this point Gore has just been introducing the concept of what global warming allegedly is and, based on his opinion, what the root cause is for global warming. He has also been endearing himself to the audience through his tone, his humor, illustrations, and some personal references. And I might add, he is charming, very well spoken and sounds intelligent. The average person is likely being conned by his presentation so far. But the introduction and the humor is over. Now he moves in to the serious subject matter.

Gore tells a story about a college professor that he had, named Roger Revelle. Mr. Revelle studied greenhouse gases in the 1950s, and found that the level of CO_2 in the atmosphere was growing each year. Gore then introduces a slide on the screen behind him with a picture of the globe showing North and South America. Next to the globe is a very dramatic bright red jagged line that is moving from left to right away from the globe and in a sharp upward angle, so that by the time the line reaches the edge of the screen, it has moved from the bottom of the globe to the top. There are no numbers, or any reference to scale given for the red line. However, Gore clearly states that the red line represents the growing level of CO_2 in the earth's atmosphere, and he says, "*it just keeps going up, it is relentless*".

NOTE: there is no dispute that CO_2 levels in the atmosphere are rising. However, we know that the increasing CO_2 is not directly causing an increase in the earth's temperature. That is what the snake oil salesman is trying to spin.

Next Gore with great emphasis says, "*and now we're beginning to see the impact in the real world!*" Now the real con begins.

He shows a photo of Mount Kilimanjaro (Tanzania) labeled "1970". The mountain is beautifully capped with bright snow, shrouded with clouds at lower elevations, and with lush and flowered trees in the foreground. Then he shows a photo that he says was taken "*by a friend of mine a couple of months ago*", (apparently in 2005). This photo is taken from a high elevation, possibly from an airplane. The mountain is brightly covered in sunshine, appears to have no vegetation on it at all, and the snow cap is minimal in comparison to the 1970 photo. Gore then says, "*within the decade there will be no more snows of Kilimanjaro*". It is a dramatic statement, made in a somber tone of voice. The audience is silent.

Gore is very misleading about what is happening on Mount Kilimanjaro, and he is factually incorrect. The decrease in snow cover is because of a decline in precipitation in recent years. The temperature at the summit never rises above freezing and is at an average of –7 degrees Celsius (about 19 degrees Fahrenheit). Long-term climate shifts associated with interglacial period dynamics, and exacerbated by irresponsible regional deforestation is causing the decline in the snow cap, and it has nothing to do with "global warming." The declining snow cap is being caused by sublimation (evaporation; like an ice cube shrinks in the freezer over time) and a lack of water vapor in the atmosphere, not by changing temperature. Much of the sublimation is likely due to the forests around the base of Kilimanjaro being cleared for firewood and agricultural use by the locals. If the locals had electricity they would not need to use firewood, and the trees could return, along with the evapotranspiration that keeps the up-slope winds onto the mountain flush with water vapor. We have seen the same deforestation desperation illustrated in Haiti.

Next is a photo of Glacier National Park (Montana) labeled "1910", and showing significant ice around the upper elevations of the mountain. Then he shows a photo of the same mountain region, labeled "1998", with much less ice around the top of the mountain. He then says, *"within 15 years this will be the park formerly known as glacier"*.

Next is a photo of the Columbia Glacier (Alaska), with red lines showing a pattern of glacial receding that has occurred from 1980, through 2001. Gore says, *"it just retreats every single year, and it's a shame because these glaciers are so beautiful, but those who go up to see 'em"*....and then he pauses. Then a video on the screen behind him shows an up-close view of glacier ice breaking off and collapsing into the sea, with enhanced sound heightening the drama of the spectacle.

There are two things about this illustration that indicate how misleading the snake oil salesman's message is. The first is that glacial ice "calving" into an ocean usually indicates a glacier that is advancing (growing) to the ocean, where when it meets the water, the ice will typically break off from the land based ice and fall into the water. If the ice were retreating it wouldn't fall into the water. It would just melt and recede. The second is that the earth is currently in an interglacial period, and it is during interglacial periods that nearly every glacier on the planet will retreat (melt) to varying degrees, because the global climate is warmer than during the ice age glacial period. Again, he is very dramatic and very misleading to a naïve audience.

Gore is implying that the retreat of glaciers is being driven directly by human caused global warming (CO_2 emissions). Notwithstanding the fact that CO_2 is not directly causing warming, the glacial melt worldwide has continued at a relatively uniform rate, with no acceleration resulting from the substantial increase in human CO_2 emissions in the last 50 years. The glacial melt would continue at its current rate, even if the entire world permanently reduced CO_2 emissions by 50% immediately, and permanently. Again, Gore is misleading the audience with dramatic "then and now" photos, and he is factually incorrect.

After a brief talk, supplemented with a snappy video illustration about how scientists drill ice cores from glaciers and analyze them to determine the earth's temperature as well as the CO_2 concentration in the atmosphere at points of time in history, Gore throws a graph up on the screen.

The graph shows relative temperature change from 1000 AD to 2000 AD. The graph represents degrees of temperature in Celsius, although Gore does not take the time to explain that to his audience. To do so would give a more measured understanding of the small variance in the actual temperatures being graphically depicted. Instead, the audience sees a dramatic variance between the low point temperature in 1850 AD, and the high point temperature in 2000 AD.

The difference is a total of 1 degree Celsius, which is equivalent to 1.8 degrees Fahrenheit, in a period of 150 years. Gore then takes the time to scoff at *"global warming skeptics"*, who he says "claim" that there is a *"cyclical phenomenon"*…*"but compared to what is going on now, there's just no comparison"*, Gore says.

The next very dramatic illustration is a side by side comparison of the temperature chart showing the relative change of one degree Fahrenheit from 1850 to 2000, and a chart that shows the CO_2 concentration in the atmosphere for the same time period. The CO_2 chart is scaled for PPM, which is "parts per million", however the chart only shows the range of numbers from 260 at the bottom to 380 at the top. The chart is not labeled "PPM", and Gore never mentions that, or the fact that CO_2 is a trace atmospheric gas, and that CO_2 only comprises 10% of the total greenhouse gases.

So, what happens very dramatically is that the temperature change line on the left, and the CO_2 line in the chart on the right both go dramatically straight up as they approach the right side of each chart. This is a graphic illusion and it is very misleading. Anyone who has ever worked with graphs knows that you can mislead your audience very easily, by manipulating the scaling for effect. That is what Gore did here.

Next, he completely dazzles his audience with another chart that uses the same scaling trick for effect. The chart displays

CO2 concentrations, and also displays the temperature for a period of 650,000 years. Gore says that this chart is from ice cores from Antarctica. The CO2 line on the chart is labeled (scaling) from 200 up to 400 PPM. The temperature line is labeled "Temp in F'" (Fahrenheit), however the temperature line has no scaling on the chart, so we don't know what the temperatures are, and we have no way of comparing the temperature scaling to the CO2, that is shown directly above it. However, Gore points to the temperature line on the far right of the chart which represents the most recent 50,000 years through 2005, and he says, "*in the parts of the United States that contain the modern cities of Cleveland, Detroit, and New York in the northern tier, this* (the temperature range being displayed) *is the difference between a nice day and having a mile of ice above your head*".

NOTE: the difference between "*having a nice day, and having a mile of ice above your head*" is about 80,000 years, and a rise in the average temperature of the earth of about 10 to 12 degrees Fahrenheit. That "difference" was not caused by CO2 alone, as the snake oil salesman infers to his audience. Again, Gore is being very misleading, if not outright dishonest.

Now the shock value is really demonstrated. Gore shows the red line for the CO2 going straight up from 280 PPM to 380 PPM, where it is today (that took 150 years). Gore then says, "*now if you will bear with me I would like to emphasize this point*". He then gets on a motorized scissor lift, and elevates himself into the air about 10 feet (as the audience begins to laugh at the sound of the scissor lift electric motor raising him up). This is high theater for effect, as he is elevated far above the floor to be able to point on the screen where the 380 PPM of CO2 concentration is. And it gets even better. Gore says, "*in the next 50 years it's going to continue to go up*".

The red line on the screen representing the CO2 concentration continues to go straight up, and again for effect, Gore continues to raise himself higher above the floor while standing on the scissor lift, with the rising CO2 line. The measure of the CO2 is not labeled, but it appears to be about twice as high as the current 380 PPM. The point on the screen is labeled "Projected concentration after 50 more years of unrestricted fossil fuel burning". To complete the deception, Gore reminds the audience of the temperature scale at the bottom of the screen, and he says, *"on the temperature side, if this much on the cold side is a mile of ice over our heads, what would that much on the warmer side be?"* He is referencing the scale of the CO2 line going straight up and off the chart, and implying that the temperature will do the same.

NOTE: Al Gore has implied to the audience that the alleged warming from growth in the CO2 concentration over the next 50 years, will be equivalent to what happened over 80,000 years when the glaciers of North America melted and receded back up into the far northern hemisphere. It is absurd. But because of the way that he scaled the chart (or the lack thereof), the audience does not get that explanation of the time scale.

If you were in this lecture audience, or watching this movie, and you were not informed regarding the science and the history of this issue, you would probably be convinced that global warming is going to substantially alter the climate in which you live within the next 50 years. Gore did a very convincing graphic illusion.

Now the movie moves on to showing some scenes of Gore on Capitol Hill in Washington DC. Meanwhile Gore is narrating, and he says the following: "*I have such faith in our democratic system, our self- government, I actually thought and believed that the story would be compelling enough to cause a real sea change in the way Congress reacted to that. I thought they would be startled, **and they weren't***".

So, to Mr. Gore's point here, ladies and gentlemen, the United States Congress was not impressed with Gore's opinion in the 80's when he started. The Senate was not convinced when they voted 95-0 to decline the Kyoto Protocol in 1997, and based on their lack of legislation even during the eight years of the radical progressive Obama administration, they still are not in agreement with Gore's opinion regarding global warming to this day.

For the balance of the movie Gore proceeds to explain, and illustrate, a number of imagined catastrophes, disasters and cataclysms that he predicts could happen as a result of alleged global warming, in an attempt to convince you that the apocalypse is upon humanity in the not too distant future. Gore actually calls what is going to happen, "*a collision between our civilization and the earth*". And he says the results are going to be "*like a nature hike through the book of revelations*".

Note: Nothing has happened yet, even though CO2 emissions from fossil fuels usage have been increasing for over 150 years, but never mind that! It is just going to happen, because Al Gore says so!

The first "nature hike through the book of revelations" is the speculation by Gore that global warming is causing bigger and more powerful storms. He theorizes that the alleged warming surface temperature will also result in warming ocean waters. He explains that warmer ocean waters will produce stronger and larger hurricanes. He references "a lot of big hurricanes" during the 2004 hurricane season, including hurricane Jean, hurricane Francis and hurricane Ivan. Then he says that "*the summer of 2005 was one for the books*". "*The first one was Emily that socked into Yucatan. Then hurricane Dennis came along, and it did a lot of damage*". "*And then of course came Katrina*". Gore uses

Katrina to illustrate his point that warmer ocean waters could produce larger and more intense storms. The implication is that Katrina is an example of what larger and stronger hurricanes will be like because of global warming.

Well, the problem with extrapolating Katrina to all hurricanes, or even some hurricanes is one simple and very obvious fact. Katrina made landfall in New Orleans and the Mississippi coast after traveling for four days across the Gulf of Mexico. Katrina was a category one hurricane when it crossed the lower peninsula of Florida and left the Atlantic Ocean. Then it entered the Gulf of Mexico. Within two days it grew to a category five hurricane. The reason for this rapid growth in storm intensity is that the Gulf of Mexico is significantly warmer than the Atlantic Ocean. The Gulf has an average depth of 4,800 feet, compared to the Atlantic Ocean which has an average depth of 11,000 feet. The average temperature of the Atlantic waters during hurricane season is 75 to 80 degrees. The average temperature of the waters in the Gulf of Mexico during hurricane season is 85 to 90 degrees.

There are more factors that affect the growth in intensity of a hurricane than just the temperature of the sea water. They include the barometric pressure, tropical wind patterns and a factor called wind shear. Obviously, the conditions for making a super hurricane were tragically unique in the case of hurricane Katrina, and the storm was a complete disaster for the gulf coast. While New Orleans got the most media coverage, the Mississippi coast took the direct hit from Katrina and received generationally devastating damage from the 20+ foot storm surge.

While we are on this subject, let's be clear about what happened to New Orleans in 2005. The City of New Orleans sits in a bowl, and most of the city is below sea level, with much of the city lying as much as six feet below sea level. The city is surrounded by water with Lake Pontchartrain on the north side, the Mississippi River on the south side, and to the east is the entrance to the Gulf of Mexico. The city is protected from the water by a system of man-made levees and concrete floodwalls. The potential for a failure of the levees and floodwalls due to extreme storm surge was a known risk long before we even heard the name Katrina.

The real reason that we witnessed the extensive human suffering of the poorest and most vulnerable citizens in New Orleans was due to the incompetence and lack of preparation by the city government, led by Mayor Ray Nagin. On Friday August 26, the Governor of Louisiana declared a state of emergency, and the White House deployed National Guard troops to the gulf coast region. It was not until a full 36 hours later, at 5 pm on Saturday August 27 that Mayor Ray Nagin announced a voluntary evacuation for New Orleans residents. On Sunday August 28 at 9:30 a.m. Mayor Nagin finally announced a mandatory evacuation order, with the category five hurricane Katrina less than one day from landfall. By then it was too late for the poorest residents of the city who did not have the transportation or financial resources necessary to evacuate New Orleans. Some of them went to the Super Dome, while others remained in their homes, many of whom were doomed.

Gore's implication that Katrina was caused by his theory of global warming is completely wrong and misleading. Katrina was not fueled by global warming. It was just in the warmer waters of the Gulf of Mexico with perfect wind shear conditions for four days. Here are the facts about hurricanes in the United States. During the century of 1900 to 2000, the U.S. mainland averaged two landfalls per year by a hurricane. During the ten years of 1996-2005 there were 20 hurricanes that made landfall. That is an average of two per year. During the ten years of 2006-2015 there were only eight hurricanes that made landfall in the U.S. (less than one per year). During 2006-2015 the amount of CO_2 emissions in the U.S. and worldwide continued to increase, yet the hurricane activity declined in volume and in intensity compared to the earlier decade. These facts render Gore's global warming cause and effect theory patently false.

The next "nature hike through the book of revelations" is Gore's prediction that the Arctic (northern polar region) sea ice will be entirely melted during the summer season within the next 50 to 70 years.

Gore speaking to his audience, says: "*Starting in 1970 there was a precipitous drop off in the amount and extent and thickness of the arctic ice cap. It has diminished by 40 percent in 40 years. There are two studies showing that in the next 50 or 70 years in summertime it will be completely gone. Now you might say, why is that a problem? How could the arctic ice cap actually melt so quickly? When the sun's rays hit the ice, more than 90 percent of it bounces off right back into space like a mirror. But when it hits the open ocean more than 90 percent is absorbed. As the surrounding water gets warmer, it speeds up the melting of the ice. Right now, the arctic ice cap acts like a giant mirror. All the sun's rays bounce off, more than 90 percent, to keep the earth cooler. But as it melts and the open ocean receives that sun's energy instead more than 90 percent is absorbed. So, there is a faster build-up of heat here at the North Pole in the Arctic Ocean and the Arctic generally than anywhere else on the planet. That's not good for creatures like polar bears that depend on the ice".*

The average person does not know much about the Arctic Ocean and the polar ice cap (also known as the "north pole") because it is very inhospitable, and not a tourist destination. If you just listened to Gore you might think that the Arctic is a sensitive and endangered region. Well, it is not. Here are some basic facts about the Arctic. The Arctic ice field is made up of the Greenland ice sheet and the Arctic sea ice surrounding the northern polar cap. The sea ice is the layer of ice formed on top of the Arctic Ocean when it freezes. The sea ice in the Arctic Circle covers nearly all of the Arctic Ocean during the winter. The sea ice stretches across the entire northern polar cap of the planet from Canada to Russia.

The extent of the sea ice is absolutely enormous! In the month of March when the sea ice reaches the winter maximum extent, it covers approximately 9.9 million square miles (that is 3X larger than the U.S. mainland). The Arctic winter lasts from December through March. The Arctic sea ice is not just a thin layer. The portions of the ice that do not melt during the summer season are 10 to 13 feet thick (3 to 4 meters thick).

When seawater freezes, the ice crystals growing to form the ice layer reject the salt from the ice, making the water below the ice much saltier. The difference in density between the ice and water makes the ice float. The sea ice is dynamic, and it floats around on top of the Arctic Ocean as it is pushed and pulled by winds and ocean currents. The extent of the sea ice grows in the winter and partially shrinks (melts) in the summer (the summer melt season lasts from May through August). At the end of the summer melt season, in August, the extent of the sea ice will be only about 1/2 of what it was in March. Then, come October the cycle of refreezing and growing the ice field begins again.

NASA has only been able to monitor the Arctic sea ice with satellites since 1979. The late 1970's were at the end of a 30 year cooling period. That being the case, the arctic ice cap was at its greatest extent (size) since the 1920s. So that maximum extent became the baseline for comparison when we entered the age of satellite monitoring.

The Arctic sea ice extent remained at approximately the 1979 levels until about 2004. Between 2004 and 2012 the sea ice melted at a higher than normal rate during the summer melt seasons, and the ice did not fully recover during those years in the winter refreeze. The total extent of the sea ice receded by about 10 percent when compared to the 1979 satellite image. Then, the period of receding sea ice extent ended with the winter refreeze of 2013-2014. The depleted sea ice re-grew by an area the size of Alaska, and returned to the sea ice extent range of the 1979 satellite image. Al Gore's *"diminished 40% of sea ice in 40 years"* comment is factually inaccurate.

The Arctic region has four seasons. The winter is extremely cold from November through February, with temperatures staying significantly below 0 degrees (-22 degrees to -31 degrees Fahrenheit). There is no sunlight at all during the winter (24-hour darkness). In the spring (March-April) it is still extremely cold with temperatures remaining below 0 degrees Fahrenheit, however there is sunlight during the day. In the summer (May, June, July) it warms up with a temperature range of 15 to 50 degrees Fahrenheit. The sun is up 24 hours a day during the summer. In the fall (September-October) the days get much shorter and the temperatures fall back below freezing all day. The sea ice begins the refreezing cycle during the fall. So, the Arctic region is extremely cold for 9 months of the year, including nearly 6 months of 24-hour darkness.

The next "nature hike through the book of revelations" is a real attention getter. Gore says to the audience, *"I want to focus on West Antarctica, because it illustrates two factors about land-based ice and sea-based ice. It's a little of both. It's propped on tops of islands, but the ocean comes up underneath it. So, if the ocean gets warmer, it has an impact on it. If this were to go, sea levels worldwide would go up 20 feet. They've measured disturbing changes on the underside of this ice sheet. It's considered relatively more stable, however, than another big body of ice that is roughly the same size. Greenland."*

Gore continues, *"Tony Blair's scientific advisor has said that because of what is happening in Greenland right now, the map of the world will have to be redrawn. If Greenland broke up and melted, or if half of Greenland and half of West Antarctica broke up and melted, this is what would happen"*.

He then shows animation indicating that in southern Florida the Everglades, Miami and Fort Lauderdale are under water. San Francisco Bay area is partially flooded with sea water. The southern part of Manhattan Island, including where the World Trade Center and Memorial is located, is under water.

Absurdity alert! The snake oil salesman is really laying it on thick here! This is one of the most ridiculous global warming predictions that Al Gore has ever claimed.

The Intergovernmental Panel on Climate Change (IPCC) is the UN committee that studies and provides opinions for the UN member governments about the issue of climate change (global warming). As the range of opinions in the scientific community goes, the IPCC tends to lean toward 100% man-made causing of global warming, by the emissions of CO_2. But even the IPCC doesn't go anywhere near the "whopper fish story" that Al Gore is telling here about the melting of the polar ice caps *"if West Antarctica went"*, or if *"Greenland were to go"*. These statements are entirely absurd, and Gore's credibility is eradicated by them.

The IPCC says sea-level increases up to 7 meters (23 feet) above today's levels have happened naturally in the far distant past climate, and would only be likely to happen again after several millennia (thousands of years). In the next 100 years, according to calculations based on figures in the IPCC's 2007 report, these two ice sheets between them will add a little over 6 centimeters (2.5 inches) to sea level, not 6 meters.

The fact that Gore could make these statements, and support them with dramatic animation showing the flooding of iconic American cities by sea water, and keep a straight face, is very telling of how extreme his views have become. He has no credibility left. He is essentially a religious zealot for global warming.

The next "nature hike through the book of revelations" is Al Gore's theory that the Thermohaline Circulation might be interrupted, which would cause the European continent to fall into an ice age. The thermohaline circulation is a current that runs in the oceans, and it transfers warm water from the equator to the polar regions, and then it transfers cold water back to the equator. This circulation provides warmth to the European continent, and helps to regulate the temperature of the earth. Scientists estimate that this "trip" takes about 1,600 years to complete.

In "An Inconvenient Truth" Gore explains his theory about how this critical process could be suddenly altered to the detriment of mankind. He says to the audience, *"the earth climate is like a big engine for redistributing heat from the equator to the poles. It does that by means of ocean current and wind current. They tell us, the scientists do, that the earth climate is a non-linear system. It's a fancy way they have of saying that the changes are not all just gradual. Some of them come suddenly in big jumps. On a world-wide basis, the annual average temperature is about 58 degrees Fahrenheit. If we have an increase of 5 degrees, which is on the low end of the projection, look at how that translates globally. That means an increase of only 1 degree at the equator but more than 12 degrees at the poles. So, all those wind and ocean current patterns that have formed since the last ice age and have been relatively stable, they are all up in the air and they change".*

Al Gore continues, "*one of the ones they are most worried about where they have spent a lot of time studying the problem is the North Atlantic where the Gulf Stream comes up and meets the cold wind coming off the arctic over Greenland and evaporates the heat out of the Gulf Stream and the stream is carried over to western Europe by the prevailing winds and the Earth's rotation. Isn't it interesting that the whole ocean current system is all linked together in this loop? They call it the ocean conveyor. The red are the warm surface currents, the Gulf Stream is the best known of them. The blue represents the cold currents running in the* *opposite direction. We don't see them at all because they run along the bottom of the ocean. Up in the North Atlantic, after that heat is pulled out, what's left behind is colder water and saltier water, because salt doesn't go anywhere. That makes it denser and heavier. That cold, dense heavy water sinks at a rate of 5 billion gallons per second. That pulls that current back south".* "At the end of the last ice age as the Vlad glacier was receding from North America, the ice melted and a giant pool of fresh water formed in North America. The Great Lakes are the remnants of that huge lake. An ice dam on the eastern border formed, and one day it broke. All that fresh water came rushing out, ripping open the St. Lawrence, there. It diluted the salty dense cold water, made it fresher and lighter so it stopped sinking. And that pump shut off and the heat transfer stopped, and Europe went back into an ice age for another 900 or 1000 years. The change from conditions we have here today to an ice age took place in perhaps as little as 10 years time. That is a sudden jump. Of course, that's not going to happen again, because the glaciers of North America are not there. Is there any big chunk of ice anywhere near there? Oh yeah..."* (and he points at Greenland)

So, Gore is again implying that global warming could cause Greenland to break up and melt, or half of Greenland and half of West Antarctica to break up and melt. To give you additional perspective, the Greenland ice sheet is a huge body of ice that covers 660,000 square miles, or roughly 80% of the surface of Greenland. The ice sheet is 1,500 miles long and 680 miles wide. The ice ranges in thickness from 6,600 feet (1.25 miles) to 9,800 feet (1.9 miles). The aging ice sheet is more than 10,500 feet thick at its highest point. The ice sheet has covered large parts of Greenland for the last 2 to 3 million years. It is so heavy that it has depressed the land mass underneath to below sea level. Much of the Greenland ice sheet is surrounded by mountains.

Fewer than 60,000 people live in Greenland because of the cold polar climate. Human occupation is limited to the lower latitudes in the southwest part of the island, across the Northwest Passage from far northern Canada. In the capital city of Nuuk, the temperature reaches above freezing (32 degrees Fahrenheit) only 4 months of the year. The annual average high temperature in July is 46 degrees Fahrenheit.

Eight months of the year it is below freezing, and six months of the year it is brutally cold, with average temperatures ranging between 0 degrees and 20 degrees Fahrenheit. That is in the southern end of the island that is most human habitable. Most of the island covered in ice is much colder, and is uninhabitable. Despite the manner in which Al Gore characterizes it, the Greenland ice sheet is not a delicate or sensitive environment. Greenland is located inside the Arctic circle. Greenland is not "*going to go*", as the snake oil salesman foolishly states it.

According to calculations in the IPCC's 2007 report, in the next 100 years, Greenland and Antarctica combined will add a little over 6 centimeters (2.5 inches) to sea level, meaning there will not be a sudden collapse of fresh water which is what would have to happen to interrupt the Thermohaline Circulation.

As far as the Antarctic (south pole) ice sheet is concerned, it is an even more extreme environment than the Arctic north polar region. About 98% of Antarctica is covered by the Antarctic ice sheet, a massive sheet of ice averaging at least 1.0 mile thick. The mean annual temperature of the interior of Antarctica is 57 degrees *below 0* Celsius (70.6 degrees *below 0* Fahrenheit). The coast is "warmer", though even there the summer temperature is below 0 °Celsius (32 °Fahrenheit) most of the time. This is cold beyond your ability to imagine it. Antarctica has been covered by ice for the last 15 million years.

Antarctica covers 5.4 million square miles, almost twice the size of the U.S. mainland. Antarctica is inhabited only by scientists on research projects. No-one lives in Antarctica indefinitely in the way that they do in the rest of the world, because it is so extremely cold year-round. It has no commercial industries, no towns or cities, no permanent residents. Antarctica is different from The Arctic polar region, because Antarctica is a land mass and most of the southern polar ice sits on top of the land, while the Arctic (north pole) ice is primarily floating atop the Arctic Ocean (except for the Greenland ice sheet). So, the Antarctic ice field does not grow and shrink with the seasons like the Arctic ice field does. In fact despite all of the global warming hysteria, the Antarctic ice field is actually growing. That's right, it is growing.

Al Gore's "An Inconvenient Truth" is a propaganda film. It is a dramatic and extremely misleading video that uses anecdotal illustrations that are completely factually incorrect. 100% false! Gore narrates the film with a religious fervor, and he charmingly plays on the ignorance and fear of his naïve audience. He is a snake oil salesman of the most extreme. He is malicious, and villainous.

Gore is in the process of marketing a follow up to his 2006 documentary video "An Inconvenient Truth". The new video is titled "An Inconvenient Sequel: Truth to Power". Given that every prediction that Al Gore has ever made about global warming since 1990 has proved to be wrong, the title "Truth to Power" is ironic and duplicitous. If the content of Gore's marketing campaign is indicative of what is in this follow up video, this will be another propaganda film that is even more misleading than the first.

Al Gore is shown giving a speech to an audience in which he is proclaiming that his opposition who have criticized him for claiming (in An Inconvenient Truth) that lower Manhattan would be flooded by a rise in sea levels, had been proven wrong. This is a blatant deception, and Al Gore knows it.

Gore had claimed in the first video that lower Manhattan, as well as Miami, Fort Lauderdale, the Everglades and the San Francisco Bay area would be flooded by rising sea levels that were going to be caused by the melting of the Greenland glacier, the Antarctica glacier and the Arctic sea ice. That permanent and catastrophic sea level rise has not happened. And it will not happen in the millennia.

What did happen, and what Gore is deceptively referring to is the October 2012 "Superstorm Sandy" that hit New Jersey and also impacted New York City. Hurricane Sandy began as a tropical depression in the Caribbean Sea. The storm meandered northward parallel to the U.S. east coast for six days. Hurricane Sandy was just a category one hurricane before making landfall in New Jersey. Normally a hurricane or tropical storm that stumbles into the Atlantic Ocean off the mid-Atlantic coast line late in the hurricane season will be swept out into the cold Atlantic Ocean waters where the storm will die.

Hurricane Sandy however, stumbled into an unusual jet stream pattern. The jet stream that usually flows from west to east to push weather away from the Atlantic coast had circled backed toward northern Canada, and it pulled the storm toward the Atlantic coast.

This jet stream action caused a cold air mass to approach the hurricane's warmer wind field on October 29, 2012. The leading edge of the cold air contained a low pressure center. The winds circulating around the low-pressure center of the cold air mass and of Hurricane Sandy began to mix. This interaction pulled part of the cold air mass to the south of the hurricane and contributed to pushing the storm toward a New Jersey landfall. After the cold air wrapped around and mixed with the warm air of the hurricane, the storm systems merged. This transformed the category one hurricane into a large extratropical cyclone, that was named Superstorm Sandy.

The storm brought a storm surge of 14 feet of sea water onto the shore line of New Jersey. This massive storm surge caused the Hudson River, New York Harbor, and the East River to flood the streets and tunnels of Lower Manhattan. This extraordinary hurricane storm surge flooding is what Al Gore is referring to in his claim to be vindicated for his false sea level rise prediction. This claim by Al Gore is an outright lie, and if he sticks by the claim, then Al Gore is a liar.

Let me remind Al Gore that a single storm does not make a trend, and a hurricane storm surge is not a rise in the permanent sea level. Since 1900, the U.S. mainland has averaged two landfalls per year by a hurricane. During the 10-year period of 1996 – 2005 there were a total of 20 hurricanes that made landfall (an average of 2 per year). During the 10-year period from 2006 – 2015 there were only eight hurricanes that made landfall in the U.S. The actual hurricane activity has fallen below U.S. historical averages since 2005 (11 consecutive years). The UN IPCC's Fifth Assessment Report (AR5) in 2014 denied the climate crisis narrative promoted by Al Gore, by stating: 1) *"current datasets indicate no significant observed trends in global tropical cyclone frequency over the past century"*; 2) *"no robust trends in annual numbers of tropical storms, hurricanes and major hurricane counts have been identified over the past 100 years in the north Atlantic basin"*; 3) *"there continues to be a lack of evidence of any trend of increased magnitude or frequency of flood on a global scale"*; 4) *"there* *is low confidence in detection and attribution of changes in drought over global land areas since the mid-20th century".*

Al Gore's deception in his marketing program for his new video continued. He appeared on "Fox News Sunday", during which he said "*I went down to Miami and saw fish from the ocean swimming in the streets on a sunny day. The same thing was true in Honolulu just two days ago, just from high tides because of the sea level rise now*".

Is Al Gore really that stupid? No, he is not. Al Gore knows what he said is not true. The sea level has not risen and caused fish to be in the streets. This is intentional deception.

What Al Gore is referring to in Miami and in Honolulu is called a "King Tide". King tides are a normal occurrence once or twice every year in coastal areas. The king tide is the highest predicted high tide of the year. King tides bring unusually high water levels and they can cause local tidal flooding. Tides are the rise and fall of water caused by gravitational forces of the moon and sun on the oceans of the earth. Tidal cycles contain two high tides and two low tides each day. It is entirely outrageous that Al Gore would go before a national television audience and make such a blatantly dishonest and misleading statement.

Al Gore has always been a big government liberal. He is no dummy. He has turned his global warming crusade into a multimillion dollar career. Gore is dangerous, because he misleads the impressionable Hollywood elites, and the naïve millennials. His global warming narrative fuels the Democrat party extreme left wing activists. Gore recently has even advocated the elimination of the electoral college from the United States Presidential election.

If you know anything about the constitutional history of the United States, and the concept of the separation of powers in the United States government provided by our forefathers, then you know that Al Gore's opinion has become beyond extreme. He is devoid of credibility in the scope of the foundation of liberty: The Constitution. The United States government is not a simple democracy, it is a democratic republic. The founders established the Union of the United States of America as a republic in order to avoid the tendency toward tyranny, that had befallen many prior democracies in world history. The Electoral College is designed to avoid the tyranny of a simple majority (the popular vote), and moreover to allow large and small sovereign states to exist peacefully together. Without the electoral college, the Presidential election would be biased toward just a few highly populated states. This would degrade the concept of equal representation.

Al Gore is disgraceful.

Chapter 9

The Wrap Up

Aren't you relieved and happy to know that you are not going to be the downfall of the planet? You, just by driving your car and keeping your home comfortable, simply by living your life, are not destroying the earth's climate. I can't imagine the sadness, frustration and fear caused by living with the guilt of believing what Al Gore, the UN climatologists and the liberal mainstream press keep repeating about anthropogenic global warming. It is a cruel false narrative that they are blaming on you and me, and our fellow citizens of the world.

There has only been mild warming of the climate since the industrial revolution began (1820). There has been no warming since 1997 (20 years) even though one-third of all human CO2 emissions in modern history have occurred since 1997.

There is no empirical evidence of a significant warming in the Arctic Ocean or of any sustained loss of the Arctic sea ice. There will be no commercial shipping in Canada's Northwest Passage even during the summer months, due to the extent and thickness of the Arctic sea ice. There has been no change in the global frequency, strength or duration of hurricanes, cyclones, floods, or droughts worldwide. There is no empirical evidence indicating that sea level rise is accelerating beyond the average experienced in the last century. Not one of the prior climate disaster predictions has ever become reality. Nor will they in the future.

The so-called "climate crisis" exists only in the computer climate models of the UN scientists. The stated objective of the UNFCCC is to "*stabilize greenhouse gas concentrations in the atmosphere at a level that would prevent dangerous anthropogenic (i.e., human-induced) interference with the climate system*". With that simple charter statement from the UN charter for the IPCC, the UN eliminated any illusion of objectivity of the IPCC. The United Nations Intergovernmental Panel on Climate Change is a biased and dishonest single purpose organization that is using the legitimate field of science to create a false narrative of exclusively anthropogenic global warming, whose goal is an international treaty that would mandate requirements on its member nations, that will result in taxation and other life altering modifications on the innocent citizens of the member nations. The primary target is the United States.

Despite all the predictions of climate disasters to come from alleged anthropogenic global warming, NO government has *ever* agreed to be subject to any legally binding regulations regarding the control of the growth of, or the decrease in, CO_2 emissions. The U.S. Senate voted 95-0 in 1997 to reject an international treaty (the Kyoto Protocol) regarding CO_2 emissions. The United Nations Intergovernmental Panel on Climate Change (UN IPCC) stated in May 2007 that "*governments must act quickly to force through changes across all sectors of society*". The UN knows that there is no climate crisis, and that only through authoritarian force can they hope to tax Americans.

The earth has managed to start and end four massive ice ages that lasted tens of millions of years each during the last 2.4 billion years, all before there was any human existence on the planet. Any correlation that exists between human emissions of CO_2 and the earth's temperature variance, is being over-powered by counter-acting natural processes within the earth's climate, as well as some very powerful outside forces that are acting on the planet from the solar system.

The fundamental job of the earth's climate is to get rid of excess heat. The "earth's weather" is a very powerful atmospheric circulation system. The combination of the heat and energy consumption by evaporation and evapotranspiration, and the climate cooling effects of the global weather systems are cumulatively stronger than the greenhouse warming effect.

There is no "consensus" in the scientific community about global warming. In science consensus is irrelevant. The work of science has nothing to do with consensus.

Liberals are pushing a scandalous attempt to exert control over the American citizens use of fossil fuels, right along with and in full support of the UN's efforts. Redistribution of wealth is a central tenant of liberalism. Global warming, or militant environmentalism, is about the agenda of the leftist liberal activists internationally, and the radical left of the Democrat party in the U.S., to control the destiny of the American people. It is about power, influence, and money.

The global warming activists have a batting average of 0.000 in the predictions of global warming calamities. They literally have not gotten a single prediction right in 50 years. That is because there is NO global warming climate crisis.

Global warming is a hoax.

End of Story.